WRITINGS BY JOEL S. GOLDSMITH

All titles listed above can be found at www.JoelGoldsmithBooks.com.

A NEW HORIZON

RECOMMENDED CHAPTERS OF
THE INFINITE WAY

Joel S. Goldsmith

Acropolis Books, Publisher
Longboat Key, Florida

A NEW HORIZON
RECOMMENDED CHAPTERS OF THE INFINITE WAY

© 2024 by Acropolis Books
All rights reserved.

For information contact:
Acropolis Books, Inc.
Longboat Key, Florida
http://www.joelgoldsmithbooks.com

Book design by Palomar Print Design

Cover image: "Sunset with Crab Fishermen"
by Hendrik Willem Mesdag (1902)

Goldsmith, Joel S., 1892-1964.
A new horizon: recommended chapters of the infinite way / Joel S. Goldsmith.
    p. cm.

ISBN 978-0-87491-007-0

Except the Lord build the house,
they labour in vain that build it.

Psalm 127

Illumination dissolves all material ties and binds men together with the golden chains of spiritual understanding; it acknowledges only the leadership of the Christ; it has no ritual or rule but the divine, impersonal universal Love; no other worship than the inner Flame that is ever lit at the shrine of Spirit. This union is the free state of spiritual brotherhood. The only restraint is the discipline of Soul; therefore, we know liberty without license; we are a united universe without physical limits; a divine service to God without ceremony or creed. The illumined walk without fear – by Grace.

The Infinite Way

TABLE OF CONTENTS

A NEW HORIZON

RECOMMENDED CHAPTERS OF
THE INFINITE WAY

INTRODUCTION

DURING JOEL GOLDSMITH's worldwide teaching and healing ministry, he was often asked by students what to study and how to study. Over and over, Joel recommended eight specific chapters in the various writings that he knew summarized the essential teachings of The Infinite Way. In chapter ten of *The Contemplative Life*, he writes, "In order to build a consciousness of truth, all Infinite Way students should know the following passages as well as they know their own names." He emphasized that these chapters are of paramount importance to serious seekers because they contain answers to almost every problem that presents itself to the student, including family relations, illness, and supply. We are pleased and privileged to be able to offer these important chapters to our readers in one volume.

The first chapter is "The New Horizon" in *The Infinite Way*. Joel writes that all the principles necessary for developing the healing consciousness are in this chapter, which he called "the practitioner's chapter,"—meaning those who understand and then embody the principles within the chapter hold the keys to the healing, teaching, and sharing way of life.

Next is chapter two, "Break the Fetters that Bind You" from *The 1958 Infinite Way Letters* [now included in *The Heart of Mysticism, Vol. V*]. This chapter presents an entire lesson on the hypnotic nature of the universal beliefs that we accept unconsciously simply by being born into a specific frame of life. In this profound chapter, Joel outlines how we may break out of these invisible limitations of the "human scene" by knowing and experiencing life in one's own Christ-being—limitless and full of wonder.

In chapter three, "Protection" from *The 1955 Infinite Way Letters* [now included in *The Heart of Mysticism, Vol. II*], you find the principles of one power, impersonalization, and nothingization; these are the core principles of spiritual healing as practiced in The Infinite Way. This essential chapter addresses key questions: How can I prevent the conditions that later need healing? How do I protect myself or my family or community from the uncertainties of life? It explains that anything negative that befalls us—illness, accident, loss, discord in human relationships—happens because we have not learned the principles of protective work.

Chapter four, "Contemplation Develops the Beholder" from *The Contemplative Life*, is a comprehensive masterclass on contemplation. It answers: What is contemplation? How is it practiced, and why? A life of contemplative meditation is both a path forward and inward. This chapter envisions the life of "praying without ceasing," which is a life that is at once practical but always deeply inspiring and illuminating.

The fifth chapter, "The Relationship of Oneness" in *The Art of Spiritual Healing*, is one of two chapters in this volume addressing relationships. It is also one of the most important chapters in The Infinite Way writings because it lays out a key principle of The Infinite Way message: "Your world is embodied in your consciousness; it reflects the state of your consciousness because your consciousness governs your world." It gives specific ways to treat daily concerns, whether with the family, community, or the world.

Chapter six, the "Introduction" in the book *Practicing the Presence*, invites "every person who has known dissatisfaction, incompleteness, and frustration..." to the ultimate discovery of true Self, which is a Presence within that is "...nearer than breathing, closer than hands and feet." This chapter opens the door to the adventure of "practicing the Presence."

Chapter seven, "Love Thy Neighbor," also from *Practicing the Presence,* is Joel's seminal outpouring of instruction about relationships, focusing on all aspects of love.

Chapter eight, "God is One" from *Living the Infinite Way,* illuminates a prerequisite teaching of The Infinite Way message: "There is no selfhood apart from God since God appears as this universe..." This chapter highlights that "God *is*" and "God appears *as*...your being and my being." Joel felt these two words— "is" and "as"—were the two most important words in the teaching.

As Joel emphasized, these eight chapters embody the essential principles of The Infinite Way of life. In working with them, studying them, and coming to know them "as well as you know your own name," the seeds of truth will sprout and develop a whole new consciousness within you.

IMPORTANT EDITOR'S NOTE

We have added an important bonus chapter in this collection—one that has become a classic in The Infinite Way writings: Chapter nine, "No *And!*" from *The Realization of Oneness.*

In a talk given in Hawaii in 1964, Joel previewed the upcoming *April Monthly Letter* for distribution to students worldwide. "Our monthly 1964 Letter will constitute another textbook of Infinite Way practice, and in the April *Letter*...you will find the basic, unique principles of The Infinite Way—I would rather say the essence of them—in about as condensed a form as I have ever seen them." Later in the talk, he emphasized, "The entire year is going to be devoted to the healing ministry, but these two months, April and May, are actually the condensed healing principles that are unique to this message."[*]

This *Letter* of April 1964 appeared as the chapter "No *And!*"[**] in the book *Realization of Oneness,* which was published after Joel passed in June 1964, and we felt these direct words of Joel's were his "stamp of approval" to include this beloved chapter in *A New Horizon.*

---

[*] From the 1964 Oahu/Maui Series, recording 546B: "Between Two Worlds—Material Sense, Spiritual Discernment."

[**] Also of note: The chapter "No *And!*" as well as the 1964 *April Monthly Letter,* were based on an early Honolulu class from 1952-12A: "The Thunder of Silence."

I

THE NEW HORIZON

THE SENSE WHICH presents pictures of discord and inharmony, disease and death, is the universal mesmerism which produces the entire dream of human existence. It must be understood that there is no more reality to harmonious human existence than to discordant world conditions. It must be realized that the entire human scene is mesmeric suggestion, and we must rise above the desire for even good human conditions. Understand fully that suggestion, belief, or hypnotism is the substance, or fabric, of the whole mortal universe and that human conditions of both good and evil are dream pictures having no reality or permanence. Be willing for the harmonious as well as the inharmonious conditions of mortal existence to disappear from your experience in order that reality may be known and enjoyed and lived.

Above this sense-life, there is a universe of Spirit governed by Love, peopled with children of God living in the household or temple of Truth. This world is real and permanent: Its substance is eternal Consciousness. In it there is no awareness of discords or even of temporary and material good.

The first glimpse of Reality—of the Soul-realm—comes with the recognition and realization of the fact that all temporal conditions and experiences are products of self-hypnotism. With the realization that the entire human scene—its

1

good as well as its evil—is illusion, comes the first glimpse and taste of the world of God's creation and of the sons of God who inhabit the spiritual kingdom.

Now, in this moment of uplifted consciousness, we are able, even though faintly, to see ourselves free of material, mortal, human, and legal laws. We behold ourselves separate and apart from the bondage of sense, and in a measure, we glimpse the unlimited boundaries of eternal life and of infinite Consciousness. The fetters of finite existence begin to fall away; the price tags begin to disappear.

We no longer dwell in thought on human happiness or prosperity, nor is there any longer concern about health or home. The "wider, grander view" is coming into focus. The freedom of divine being is becoming apparent.

The experience, at first, is like watching the world disappear over a horizon and drop down from before us. There is no attachment to this world, no desire to hold onto it—probably because to a great extent the experience does not come until a great measure of our desire for the things of "this world" has been overcome. At first we cannot speak of it. There is a sense of " 'Touch me not; for I am not yet ascended'—I am still between the two worlds; do not touch me or make me speak of it because it may drag me back. Let me be free to rise; then, when I am completely free of the mesmerism and its pictures, I will tell you of many things which eyes have not seen nor ears heard."

A universal illusion binds us to earth—to temporal conditions. Realize this, understand this, because only through this understanding can we begin to lessen its hold upon us. The more fascinated we are with conditions of human good and the greater our desire for even the good things of the flesh, the more intense is the illusion. In proportion as our thought dwells on God, on things of the Spirit, the greater the freedom from limitation we are gaining. Think neither on the discords nor on the harmonies of this world. Let us not fear the evil nor love the good of human existence. In proportion as we accomplish this, is the mesmeric influence lessening in our experience. Earth ties begin to disappear; shackles of limitation fall away; erroneous conditions give place to spiritual harmony; death gives way to eternal life.

The first glimpse into the heaven of here and now is the beginning of the ascension for us. This ascension is understood now as a rising above the conditions and experiences of "this world," and we behold the "many mansions" prepared for us in spiritual Consciousness—in the awareness of Reality.

We are not bound by the evidence of the physical senses; we are not limited to the visible supply; we are not circumscribed by visible bonds or bounds; we are not tied by visible concepts of time or space. Our good is flowing from the infinite invisible realm of Spirit, Soul, to our immediate apprehension. Let us not judge our good by any so-called sensible evidence. Out of the tremendous resources of our Soul comes the instant awareness of all that we can utilize for abundant living. No good thing is withheld from us as we look above the physical evidence to the great Invisible. Look up, look up! The kingdom of heaven is at hand!

I am breaking the sense of limitation for you as an evidence of *My* presence and of *My* influence in your experience. *I*—the *I* of you—am in the midst of you revealing the harmony and infinity of spiritual existence. *I*—the *I* of you—never a personal sense of "I"—never a person—but the *I* of you—am ever with you. Look up.

II

BREAK THE FETTERS
THAT BIND YOU

MANY OF THE difficulties and struggles in our experience come because we are living on different planes of consciousness, sometimes on one and sometimes on another, and often these planes are in conflict one with another. On one plane we are physical beings with minds, the body being the dominant factor; on another plane we are mental beings with bodies, that is, we are a mind and a body, and the body is governed by the mind. It may be governed by a conscious activity of mind or it may be by an involuntary activity of mind.

In recent months, there have been many accounts in magazines and newspapers of the experiments which have been conducted in the area of subliminal perception through the mediums of television and motion picture. In the first experiments, which were held inside a moving picture theatre, the audience was instructed to go into the lobby during the intermission to buy popcorn and Coca-Cola. Even though they did not know such a suggestion had been given to them, because the slide had been flashed across the screen so rapidly that it was invisible to the eyes and, therefore, did not register consciously in the mind, the majority of those in the theatre were impelled to obey this suggestion. Whether or not they wanted the popcorn or

Coca-Cola made no difference. The impulsion was so strong that they felt compelled to go out and buy it, giving their good money for something they may not have wanted and otherwise would not have bought. It was not necessary for them to be aware of the suggestion, to see or to hear it, and there was no knowledge that it was even being made.

If a person is not alert, he will obey such subtly given instructions because this technique is not aimed at the conscious mind; it is aimed at the subconscious. These experiments show the extent to which the body obeys the dictates of the mind. On the human level of consciousness, that is exactly what happens. The body is subject to the mind. On this same level of consciousness, there are certain laws, mental and physical, which if violated bring punishment. This is the law of cause and effect: "Whatsoever a man soweth, that shall he also reap"—as you do to others so will it be done unto you. All this is because, as human beings, we live on a mental plane, and even the body is subject to mental control.

The Mind, Ignorant of Truth,
Is an Easy Prey to World-Beliefs

Every discord is the result of the violation of some law on the human plane, mental or physical. If there were no violation of law, there would be no inharmony—no disease, no sin. Some kind of a law is always being violated: Sitting in a draft or getting the feet wet results in catching cold; exposure to contagion results in disease; injudicious eating results in functional disorders. These are mental laws which have been laid down, and just as the subject in the experiments with subliminal perception is unaware of the suggestions being thrust at him, so it is not necessary to know these mental and physical laws to be affected by them and to suffer the penalty their violation brings.

There are thousands of laws of which people may be unaware, and yet when they are violated, a penalty follows: A newborn child may know nothing of the ill effects of drafts, but if he happens to be in a draft, he is likely to catch cold. Obviously, an infant would know nothing of the existence of such a law, but it is not necessary to know that there is a law or that it is being violated in order to come under its penalty.

All the error in this world is as universal and as invisible as the slides flashed upon the screen in the experiments with subliminal perception, and it operates in the same manner—without a conscious awareness of it. That makes everybody a victim of it. As a matter of fact, everybody born into this world is a victim of all the unknown laws lodged in human consciousness. Almost from the moment of conception, a person's consciousness is being filled with beliefs of power in people and conditions, and his acceptance of these beliefs makes him a victim of them.

Hawaiians know that the work of the good and bad kahunas is effective primarily because of individual fear or belief in their power. The aborigines of Australia engage in much the same practice under the name of black magic, and whereas the kahuna in Hawaii might cast his spell with a piece of fingernail or a hair, the black magician of the aborigines accomplishes the same results by pointing. He either points his finger or a sharp piece of wood in the direction of the victim, and the moment he does that, his victim becomes ill and in a few days dies. Why? Certainly not because there is any power in kahunaism and not because there is any power in black magic, but only because they have been accepted and feared as a power. Sin and disease operate in the world in the same way as kahunaism does—by suggestion. We do not have to know that the suggestion has been made; we only have to believe that the thoughts and things of the world are power.

Originally, metaphysical healing rested on the principle of truth dispelling error or truth over error. The basic idea was that if evil thoughts entertained in the mind had an effect on the body, how much greater an effect would good thoughts have on the body. On that theory, a religion sprang up—the religion of right thinking. It is founded on the idea that, under ordinary circumstances, the human race is a victim of whatever beliefs are circulating in consciousness. For example, if an epidemic is rampant in one part of the world, it soon spreads throughout the world because, according to adherents of this teaching, wherever there are people to think, there are people to accept the result of thought. Metaphysicians argued that if people throughout the world are an easy prey to erroneous suggestions, truth or right thinking should have an equally great effect upon the body, only it would be of a beneficial nature.

Out of this teaching in which the individual filled his consciousness with truth, which acted therapeutically upon the body and which was found to be very effective, grew psychosomatic medicine, founded on similar principles. It used psychological healing, that is, changing the patient's attitude from a negative to a positive base, a technique of filling consciousness with truth as against having it filled with erroneous beliefs and theories. A mind imbued with error, wrong thinking or negative thinking, produces a negative condition of body, pocketbook, or of family life; a mind imbued with truth results in a healthy body, a healthy purse, or a healthy family life. In other words, it is a question now of deciding whether one is going to wake up in the morning and accept any or every thought that comes to him, or whether he is going to take a positive stand and reject the negative.

This type of practice has been a step in the right direction because it has been a movement away from leaving one's mind a blank for the world to act upon. If a person has a mind which merely accepts everything that is given to it orally, visually, or invisibly, that mind can be acted upon and made to follow the dictates of an imposed thought—of suggestion. The individual who has determined that he will do his own thinking and will be moved or governed only by what he, himself, accepts has started on a new path. The effects of world-belief become less of a dominating factor in such a person's experience. Truth-students, regardless of which truth-teaching they may follow, are less frequently victims of this universal mesmerism than is the world at large, and furthermore, they are less affected by the conditions of the world.

Refuse to Accept World-Beliefs as Power

Everyone must learn to awaken in the morning and take hold of his own mind by realizing:

Nothing can enter my mind from without because my mind is an instrument through which I function—not an instrument through which somebody else functions or through which world-belief functions. My mind is an instrument given to me just as my body is given to me, and just as I keep my body inviolate so I keep my mind inviolate, free from world-beliefs. I do not permit my mind to be used by suggestion, by outside influences, or by outside opinions or theories. I make my mind an instrument for the truth of God. My mind is an instrument through which I function.

This realization cannot be achieved through a blind faith that God will take care of us. It must be done consciously. If we are to be saved from these world-influences, these mesmeric influences like disease and death, it is not going to be God who is going to save us from them. It will be because we refuse to let our mind be acted upon by world-beliefs and hold our mind open only to God.

If we dwell—live, move, and have our being—in the secret place of the most High, none of the evils of the world will come nigh our dwelling place. They will not happen to us if we are living in obedience to the principle of keeping consciousness filled with truth, if we are refusing to accept world-beliefs as power and are realizing that the only power operating within us is the power of truth. Whether or not we consciously know a specific truth is not the point. The point is whether or not we know that the truth operating in our consciousness is power and that nothing else is.

Among many truth-students, there is too much superstition, far too much blind faith that there is some kind of a God who does something for metaphysical students that He does not do for other people. That is a fatal belief. God is God, and God is no respecter of persons. God is available to white or black, Jew or Christian, Mohammedan or Hindu. God is available to anyone on the face of the globe, to anyone who makes himself consciously one with Him. It has nothing to do with God. The question is whether an individual believes that he is living as a human being in a world where hypnotism—a kind of subliminal perception— has been going on for generations, going on unknown to us as individuals, yet operative in our consciousness or in what the psychologists now call the subconscious; or whether he recognizes that his mind is not subject to the suggestions and vagaries of world-beliefs, but is a transparency through which God functions.

Seventy-five to eighty years of metaphysical practice prove that ninety percent of the world's errors can be avoided in proportion as we take hold of ourselves and consciously, consciously recognize no power but one, and that power not external to us, operating upon us, but within us, operating outward from us. The room in which we are sitting at this very moment may be filled with all the error that exists anywhere in the world. At this very moment, it may be filled with the atmosphere of death, disease, accident, sin, and false appetite. These suggestions are not only pouring in from the radio and television, but they are pouring in through the world-consciousness. Not knowing this, we may become victims of them in one form or another, but knowing it, we can protect ourselves from their effects.

Watch what happens in your own experience when you learn to awaken in the morning and absolutely bar from yourself the possibility of world-thought entering your consciousness and operating in your experience. "Ye shall know the truth, and the truth shall make you free." "A thousand shall fall at your left hand and ten thousand at your right hand," but it shall not come nigh those who dwell in this truth. There have always been wars and rumors of wars; there have been plagues, droughts, floods, and storms; and yet Scripture says that none of these things "shall come nigh your dwelling place." Anyone who is willing to go to the trouble of giving sufficient time every day to the recognition that even though world-beliefs exist they do not exist as power can experience a measure of this immunity promised in Scripture:

World-beliefs can find no entrance into my consciousness because my consciousness is Truth expressing Itself. No human theories, beliefs, laws, or hypnotic suggestions can enter my consciousness to defile or to make a lie. All power—the power of Good, or God—flows out from within me to this world.

Hypnotism is not truth, and if we learn to abide in spiritual truth and apply that truth to every experience of daily living, negative thoughts and things that operate in the world through universal mesmerism will be nullified. As long as our consciousness is filled with truth, we cannot be made to accept a lie. When we maintain our mind as a temple of God and let nothing enter that mind except what comes from God, we shall find that we are living in inner peace.

Whether that human experience will be harmonious or inharmonious, whether it will be successful or unsuccessful, whether it will be good or evil, is determined by us. We determine that by our willingness to set aside some part of every hour to remind ourselves that we are not victims of whatever it is that is floating around in the air, whether thoughts or things, but that we are the outlet for the presence and power of God. Our mind is the temple of God, just as is our body, and we maintain its sanctity.

Everyone on the human plane is acting and reacting to some suggestion of universal belief. Humanly, we are antennas and respond to another person's thoughts, moods, and disposition; we react to one another's feelings as well as to world-feelings and world-tensions. When other people fear something collectively or individually, we fear the same thing; but once we recognize that tendency, we become less and less responsive to outside influences. A person who does not understand that there are unseen forces governing his human experience would, of course, be unwilling to spend even five minutes of his time in an effort to become immune to world-beliefs. But once we begin to perceive that there are many things that we do that we do not really intend doing or do not want to do, and that we think many thoughts that are contrary to our nature and which must have been imposed upon us from without, then we shall begin to see that there is a universal mesmerism and we shall be willing to make the effort necessary to free ourselves from it:

Universal mesmerism is not a power that can enter my consciousness; it seems to be a power and acts like a power only because of my ignorance of its nature. Now that I recognize it for what it is, I no longer respond to it, I no longer accept its suggestions, I no longer react to it. I am the temple of the living God, and all that the Father is flows through me.

Attaining the Higher Dimension of Life

There is another plane of consciousness which Jesus referred to as "*My* kingdom." This is the plane of consciousness in which The Infinite Way functions in your life after you have assimilated and proved in some measure the correct letter of truth as taught in our writings and recordings. Without the attainment of the knowledge of the correct letter of truth and its proof in your experience, it is almost impossible to attain the spirit of Truth, the actual consciousness of Truth, which is the "My kingdom"—the spiritual kingdom, or Consciousness.

"My kingdom is not of this world"—not of the mental and physical world. In this kingdom, there is a peace that can never be known with the mind or body: "My peace I give unto you: not as the world giveth, give I unto you." This is an entirely different realm of consciousness. In this higher consciousness, there is only being: There are no laws; there is no cause and no effect; there is neither good nor evil, up nor down. There is just being. Strangely enough when "My kingdom" or "My peace" can be brought even into the mind, it nullifies human law and removes the penalties for its transgression because it removes the transgression itself. Watch the change which occurs when you make yourself consciously one with God, when you open yourself and become a state of receptivity to everything that flows from the kingdom of God within, thereby consciously shutting yourself off from the world's mesmeric influence.

The higher dimension of life to which the Master referred as "My kingdom" is not accessible to the person who is under world-mesmerism. As that mesmerism is dispelled, and we become as conscious of God operating in us as we were conscious of fear, doubt, suspicion, hate, envy, jealousy, we become susceptible to the activity of the kingdom of God. Those who understand how world-mesmerism, or universal hypnotism, operates can nullify its effects in their experience.

It is folly for a human being whose eyes are not open and who does not perceive clearly the nature of this universal sense to think that, by going through the forms of meditation, he is going to hear the still small voice. It is folly for the person who is still indulging in personal sense—hate, envy, jealousy, malice, prejudice—to believe that he can sit down, close his eyes, and immediately God will be on the scene to protect him. This is not possible until a person has separated himself from the very influences that originally created a sense of separation from God. We are only separated from God because the mind, instead of being a clear transparency for the Soul, has become clouded by personal sense or world-mesmerism. In such a state of hypnotism, God cannot be heard.

Non-Reaction Is the Measure of Our Freedom from World-Beliefs

We can help each other over many and many a hard place, but this can only be done to the extent that we are no longer being used by personal sense, by a universal hypnotism, which fills our minds, thoughts, and even bodies with world-beliefs. It takes months before we can separate ourselves from these universal beliefs and become receptive and responsive to the "still small voice" within; but after a few weeks of practice, we begin to be less and less receptive and responsive to some of these world-urges. It really takes months of work, however, before we arrive at a state of consciousness which does not respond to those things which the world is fearing, which is indifferent to certain things which, heretofore, aroused anger, resentment, rebellion, or a desire for revenge, or which does not react to greed, selfishness, or sensuality.

Learn this lesson well! The human world and the people in it are victims of world-mesmerism—victims of every negative, diseased, sinful, and poverty-stricken state of thought that operates as human consciousness—and it strikes at us wherever we are weakest. If it is a fear of disease, world-mesmerism will take the form of some kind of illness; if it is a fear of lack, world-mesmerism will take the form of poverty or limitation; if it is false appetite, world-mesmerism will take the form of alcoholism, drug-addiction, or even gluttony: World-mesmerism will always find its way to our most vulnerable—our weakest—spot. If nothing else, it will make us fear a ghost somewhere.

Our work as students is to obey the Master's injunction to come out and be separate: "I pray not that thou shouldest take them out of the world, but that thou shouldest keep them from the evil. They are not of the world, even as I am not of the world." When we are responding less and less to the world's impulses and the world's fears, the world's doubts, and the world's sin, lacks, and diseases; when we have more and more immunity; when we go through life less and less aware that those things are going on around us, or if we are aware of them, they make no impression upon us; then we know that we are being freed from world-mesmerism and are now in the world but not of it. We are now of the kingdom of God. Now the still small voice can take over and direct us and lead us into green pastures, beside the still waters; now the inner spiritual impulse can do those things for us which Scripture promises.

No one can do this for us. We alone can free ourselves of the hypnotism of this world. When we ask for help from a practitioner, the practitioner can give us help on that particular problem at that particular minute. A practitioner may nullify some form of error or break some form of hypnotism for us, however, only to make room for other forms. Why? Because we have not freed ourselves from the invisible influence that exists as universal hypnotism.

Hypnotism Is Not a Power

Do not make the mistake, however, of fearing this invisible influence, for it is not a power except to those who are either ignorant of it or to those who give it power. It is not a power once its nature is realized. At this stage of our experience, we should be able to shut ourselves out from world-hypnotism just as we can turn our radio to any station we want or turn it off completely. It may take us a few months or longer to arrive at this stage of consciousness, but it can only be accomplished if it is practiced faithfully many times a day.

When something says, "I have a headache," our immediate response must be, "No, it is not I who have a headache. This is universal sense striking at me." Or if the suggestion comes, "I have a lack that I cannot fill," the answer is, "No, it is not I who have the lack. I am accepting a universal sense of lack." We shall not only be in the world but of it until we break the hypnotic sense that makes us the victim of this silent thing that is going on.

For thousands of years, the human race has believed things that are not true: the world was flat; the sun revolved around the earth; wars and pestilence were necessary to decrease the population so that the population would not exceed the forseeable food supply. Then some enlightened person—someone with vision—was able to see beyond the appearance and disprove some theory which heretofore had been accepted as law—astronomical, geographic, economic, medical, or dietary.

We do not have to accept limitation in any form—limitation of health, of pocketbook, or of human relationships. We do not have to accept limitation in any form because these limitations are merely man-made beliefs which have no more foundation than the many theories which at one time were considered sound but which today are dismissed as ludicrous. We must stand on the truth that I and the Father are one and all that the Father has is ours. We must realize our infinity and prove it. But this can only be demonstrated as we realize that we have been victimized, not by lack, but by a universal suggestion which we have ignorantly accepted.

Much of the foregoing comes under the heading of what we call protective work, but that is a misnomer because the term "protective work" implies that there is some power from which to be protected. What we need to be protected from is our ignorance of our true identity, our ignorance of the source of true wisdom. Many of the things we believe are not true at all; many of the things we believe about each other and many of the things we believe about the world are not true at all. As one writer said almost a hundred years ago, "The trouble with people is not that they don't know, but that they know so much that ain't so." In order to know how much blasphemy and how much bearing of false witness against our neighbor there is in the world, it is only necessary to travel and meet people of the world. They are not at all what the world would have us believe they are.

We must stop accepting world-hypnotism. We must realize that we have been accepting what the world pumps into us silently and invisibly, accepting it as if it were fact, instead of turning to God and letting God reveal the truth: "Father, what is the truth about this individual or this condition?"

Usually, when we do this in humility and sincerity, the answer will come back, "This is My child, My beloved child in whom *I* am well-pleased. This is My temple."

On the whole, what we believe about each other is not true. It is what is revealed to us from within that comes with authority, and that will come only when we have sufficiently come out from among them and become separate:

Nothing can enter my being that defileth or maketh a lie for I and the Father are one. I am subject only unto the law and life of God, the wisdom of God, the mind of God, the soul of God. I am in the midst of me, and from that I comes my wisdom, my direction, my guidance, my protection, my sustenance. I turn only to It and I am led and fed by It.

III

PROTECTION

IN THE MATERIAL sense of life, the word "protection" brings up the thought of defense or armor, a hiding place from an enemy, or some sense of withdrawal from danger. In the mental sciences, protection refers to some thought or idea or some form of prayer that would save one from injury or hurt from an outside source. In the use of the word "protection," thought is immediately drawn to the fact that existing somewhere is a destructive or harmful activity or presence or power and that protection, by word or thought, is a means of finding security from this danger to one's self or one's affairs.

In The Infinite Way, we have learned that God is One: therefore, God is one power, and we live in that conscious oneness. The moment the idea of God as One begins to dawn in consciousness, we understand that in all this world, there is no power and no presence from which we need protection. You will see this as you dwell on the word "Omnipresence," and realize that in this all-presence of good you are completely alone with a divine harmony—a harmony which pervades and permeates consciousness, and is in itself the allness and the onlyness of good.

Ponder this idea and meditate upon it, and note how the revelation and assurance come to you, within your own being, that this is true: there is but One, and because of the

19

nature of that One, there is no outside influence for either good or evil. There is no presence or power to which to pray for any good that does not already exist as Omnipresence, right where you are. In your periods of communion, note the assurance that comes with the realization that God alone *is*, and that God's presence is infinite. There is no other power; there is no other presence; there is no destructive or harmful influence in any person, place or thing; there is no evil in any condition. God could not be One and yet find an existence separate and apart from that One. God alone is being—think of that—*God alone is Being*. How then can you pray to God in word or thought, or how can you defend yourself, mentally or physically, in the realization of God as being the one and the only Being?

The Master has told us: "There is nothing from without a man, that entering into him can defile him: but the things which come out of him, those are they that defile the man." Our studies and meditations have revealed that whatever of discord or inharmony is manifest in our experience today is coming through the activity of our own thought. We have accepted the universal belief of a power, a presence, and an activity apart from God; we have accepted the belief that some one or some thing, outside of our own being, can be a presence or power for evil in our experience; and the acceptance of this rather universal belief causes much of our discord and inharmony.

As we consciously bring ourselves back, day after day, day after day, to the actual awareness of God as infinite Being, God manifesting and expressing Itself as our individual being, we understand more fully that all power flows out from us, through us, as a benediction and blessing to the world, but that no power acts upon us from without our own being. As students of The Infinite Way, it must become clear to us that there is no power acting upon us from without our own being for either good or evil. Just as we have learned that the stars, the creations of God in the heavens, cannot act upon us in accord with astrological belief, so we have learned that conditions of weather, climate, infection, contagion, or accident, likewise, cannot act injuriously upon those who have come into some measure, at least, of the understanding of the nature of God and the nature of individual being. We are constantly being reminded to become more and more aware of the nature of God, the nature of prayer, and the nature of individual being so that we will understand ourselves as the offspring of God, of whom it is truly said, "Son, thou art ever with me, and all that I have is thine."

All of human existence is made up of the belief of two powers—the good and the evil. All religion, in its beginning, was nothing more nor less than an attempt to find something to deliver us from external conditions or powers of evil. Even today, most religions deal with a concept of God as being some kind of great power which, if we can only reach It, will protect and save us from these destructive influences which, it is claimed, exist outside our own being.

Think seriously on this subject of protection or protective work, because each day we are faced with suggestions of impending or threatened dangers. Always some person, some place, or some thing is being presented as a great danger or destructive power which we must fear, or from which we must seek a God to save us. Of course, if there were such dangers, and if there were such a God, the world would have discovered, long before this, some way to reach that God.

God's allness makes it utterly impossible for any destructive or evil influence or power to exist anywhere—in heaven,

on earth, or in hell—so do not make the mistake of thinking of God as some great power which is able to save you
from a destructive person or influence if only you can reach
Him. Do not make the common mistake of thinking that
The Infinite Way is just another method of finding God or
another manner of praying to bring God's influence into
your experience in order to overcome discord, error, evil,
sin, and disease. No—rather, understand that this message
is bringing the awareness of God as One, of God as infinite
individual being, of God as All-presence and All-power.

The universal belief in two powers, good and evil, will
continue to operate in our experience until we individually—
remember this, you and I individually—reject the belief of
two powers. In the tenth chapter of Luke, you will read that
the Master sent the seventy disciples out, "two by two, into
every city and place, whither he himself would come." When
the seventy returned they rejoiced, saying, "Lord, even the
devils are subject unto us through thy name." But the Master
replied, "… rejoice not, that the spirits are subject unto you:
but rather rejoice, because your names are written in heaven."

In this age we need a great deal of protective thought,
but the nature of that thought must be the realization that
God's allness precludes the possibility of there ever existing
a source of evil in the world itself, or one able to operate in
individual experience. Our protective work, or our prayers
for protection, must consist of the realization that nothing
exists anywhere, at any time in our experience of the past,
present, or future, that is of a destructive nature. Through
our studies and meditations, eventually we will come to that
God-contact within us, wherein we receive the divine assurance: "Lo, I am with you alway." This will not come as a
protection against evil powers or destructive forces, but as a

continuous assurance of one Presence, one Power, one Being, one Life, one Law. It is in this awareness of oneness that we find our peace.

It would be a wonderful thing if students would take this subject of protection into daily meditation for the next month or two, saying nothing about it to anyone. Do not discuss or mention it, but just keep it a secret subject within yourselves until you arrive at a place in consciousness where you actually can feel that God is One and that the secret of protection lies not in seeking a God to save or secure you against some outside intrusion, but rather that safety, security and peace are entirely dependent on your remembrance and realization of the truth of God as One—infinite One.

Do you not see that the world is seeking peace (just as it is seeking safety and security) outside of its own being? Whereas, no peace, no safety and no security will ever be found except in our individual realization of God as One— the only Being, Presence, and Power. We cannot tell the world about peace or safety or security, but we can find it for ourselves and thereby let the world see by our experience that we have found a way higher than superstitious belief in some power of good that miraculously saves us from some power of evil. We cannot tell the world that there is no danger from outside sources, influences, or powers, but our realization of this truth can make the harmony and completeness and perfection of our lives so evident that others, one by one, will turn to seek that which we have found.

What have we found? Have we found a God to whom we can pray and from whom we can receive special favors that others, less favored, cannot receive? Have we found a God to whom we can pray and receive healing or supply or protection? No! No! We have found no such thing: we have found

God as One; we have found God as our very being. We have found God to be the Life—not a life subject to sin, disease or death, but the one and only Life; we have found God to be eternal and immortal Life, our very individual life. We have found God to be the Law—not a law that can be used to offset laws of heredity, infection, contagion or disease, but the one infinite, omnipresent Law—maintaining and sustaining the harmony and perfection of Its own creation at all times.

God is One, and beside Him there is no other. Because we know the nature of God as One, we know the nature of prayer as the realization of oneness.

> Look unto me and be ye saved, all the ends of the earth: for I am God, and there is none else.
>
> Isaiah 45:22

Spiritual Reliance

Spiritual harmony comes quickly when we have given up the desire or search for physical or outer harmony. This is the inner meaning of the Master's words: "Peace I leave with you, my peace I give unto you: not as the world giveth, give I unto you." Divine grace comes in proportion as we turn from all sense of human peace, prosperity or health, and seek the realization of "My peace," which includes the health or harmony of Spirit.

Paul tells us: "Be not deceived; God is not mocked: for whatsoever a man soweth, that shall he also reap. For he that soweth to his flesh shall of the flesh reap corruption; but he that soweth to the Spirit shall of the Spirit reap life everlasting." We must understand that in the first case, we are being warned against a faith, confidence, reliance, or dependence on the creature—that is, that which appears as effect.

However, to "sow to the Spirit," by placing one's reliance and trust and hope in the Infinite Invisible, is to reap the things of the Spirit, and in this way we honor the Creator rather than the creature. This is what the prophet Isaiah meant when he warned the Hebrews against their faith in "... the work of their own hands, that which their own fingers have made," and a deep principle is revealed in this warning.

At this point of our unfoldment, it is necessary to realize that we have left behind the law of Moses and stepped out into the grace of Truth. Surely by now we know that good humans are not rewarded by God, nor are bad humans punished by God. Whatever of reward or punishment comes into human experience comes through our own belief in such. Too often students complain bitterly about the problems they experience while on their search for God, not realizing how fortunate they are to be in the midst of these problems while seeking the revelation and realization of God, because until one has been divested of every human or material aid, one cannot know the experience of a complete reliance on the Infinite Invisible.

We are born into a world where first we learn to rely on parents, later on teachers, husbands or wives, and often we end up dependent upon our children. In between, we become dependent upon medicines and dollars so that at no time in the average person's experience does he ever learn that there is an Infinite Invisible which is far better able to supply his every need and far more dependable than any one or any thing in the visible realm. For the human, content to go through life in this way, it is naturally pleasurable to find at hand those people and things upon which he can rely, but fortunate is he if he does not come to the end of his rope and find that humans and material resources have failed him.

However, those who have set themselves on the search for God will find their journey shortened by every experience of failure on the part of friends and relatives and things because then comes the complete reliance on that which has heretofore never been experienced—the Infinite Invisible. And what spiritual treasures we can bring forth through the realization to be gained from: "My grace is sufficient for thee," and "Man shall not live by bread alone, but by every word that proceedeth out of the mouth of God."

An Important Point in Spiritual Practice

Spiritual practice, which embraces all phases of the healing work, is much more than declaring or knowing some truth after a discord has been brought to your attention. Spiritual practice is a constant, conscious realization of God as Omnipresence—of God as the life, law, substance, continuity, activity, the very soul and intelligence of all being.

Suppose at this very moment you were to receive a call asking for help, and you proceed to give a treatment, to pray, or to go into meditation or communion. If, consciously or unconsciously, you have accepted the discord and expect and hope that harmony is going to be restored through your treatment or prayer, your success will be very limited and your failures will be more numerous than your successes.

When a call comes announcing some form of discord, it is necessary to remember consciously that this is not a discord or maladjustment which, through your effort or even through God, is to be corrected, but rather that this is a specific call to know that as God was in the beginning, so God is now, and God ever will be.

Unless you are living the spiritual life in such a manner as keeps you in the realization that the past and the future are one—here and now in the present—you will find your-self in distress if a call comes saying, "My friend has just been killed: please help me." You will be in a very embar-rassing position indeed because you will be expected either to raise the dead or to accept death as an actual happening and merely give a treatment or meditation for the comfort of the bereft one. This situation must never come to you; you must never be in such a state of consciousness where anyone can announce that someone has been killed or has passed on, and then from that point, expect to do something spiritual about it.

In living the true spiritual life, you are not waiting for calls of discord and inharmony. You are living in such a state of consciousness that God alone is the reality, and your entire experience is one of dwelling in the realization of God ever governing, maintaining, and sustaining Its own universe— from the beginning of time until the end of the world.

"Before Abraham was, *I am*. I am with you alway, even unto the end of the world." This brings that past and the future into the present: if *I am* with you since before Abraham, nothing could have occurred before that call except that which was a part of the demonstration of *I am*— the all-inclusive love, presence and power of God. If *I am* with you until the end of the world, nothing can happen today, tomorrow or next week which is not a part of the all-embracing guidance, direction, and protection of the divine Principle of this universe.

In ordinary metaphysical practice, consciously or uncon-sciously, you accept the fact that there are those in the world who are suffering from discord and inharmony and that at any moment someone may telephone or come in person asking for help; if you are not very, very careful you will be tempted to give it. Unless you are already living in the consciousness of God as the omnipresent law and being, the omnipresent good, the omnipresent direction, guidance, intelligence, wisdom, substance and reality, you will automatically attempt, through spiritual means, to bring about adjustments, healings, harmonies and resurrections, all based on the fact that a sin or disease, accident or death have already occurred.

The Infinite Way is not a practice that begins with a call for help. The Infinite Way is a way of life in which, at all times, we live and move and have our being in the realization of God as Omnipresence, and in that consciousness, whenever an appearance or call of discord reaches us, we are enabled to smile in the true knowledge that no discord or inharmony has ever happened, therefore is not now in need of adjustment.

Here is one of the most important points to be achieved on the spiritual path. At one time, I was taught that practitioners should consciously and specifically know the truth every day: that all who needed me would find me. It took only twenty-four hours to learn that this was a denial of the Christ. How could I, in one breath, say, "Those who need me will find me," and in the next, when they came to me, say, "God governs you; God is your life; You are perfect now"? Do you not see that it is up to us to know, before anyone comes to us, that perfection was the true state of their being, and that perfection is the true state of their being in the here and now? Do you really believe that we have anything to do with establishing or bringing about harmony? No! No! Our place in the spiritual path is not to be repairers of damage nor resurrectors of life, nor physicians nor protective influences—that is God's function. And not only now, but from the beginning it has been God's function to be the creative

Principle of this universe, and to be the maintaining and sustaining principle unto all time.

If you understand the nature of God, you will understand that God is the creative Principle of all existence; God is the law unto all creation; God is the substance, the reality and the continuity of all creation. Therefore, all creation is in and of God, subject to God's government and God's care. It is your function to know this truth. Ye shall know this truth, and this truth will make you free—free of accepting appearances and then trying to do something about them.

Do you see wherein the message of The Infinite Way, and its practice, differs from the greater part of metaphysical teachings? Living The Infinite Way means living in the constant, conscious realization of God as infinite, omnipresent, eternal Being. It means living always in the consciousness that "before Abraham was, *I am*" the divine Principle, the protective, maintaining and sustaining influence unto this universe. It also means living in the constant, conscious realization of the truth that *I am* with you unto the end of the world, and just as nothing could happen to you yesterday, so nothing could happen to you today or tomorrow, except as a part of God's grace.

We could live lives of constant miracles if only we would abide in the consciousness of this truth: "My grace is sufficient for thee." Thy grace is sufficient for every need, but not Thy grace that is coming tomorrow. Thy grace, since before Abraham was, is my sufficiency; Thy grace is my sufficiency unto the end of the world. Thy grace of the past, present and future is at this very instant my sufficiency in all things. Every day there are temptations to believe that we or our families or students are in need of something in the nature of form (it may be food, housing, opportunity, education, employment, rest) but to all those things we can respond:

"Man shall not live by bread alone, but by every word that proceedeth out of the mouth of God," because Thy grace is man's sufficiency in every instance.

From these two scriptural passages, you can build such a consciousness of the omnipresence of the Infinite Invisible that forever after, you will learn to love and enjoy and appreciate everything in the world of form and everything that exists as effect, yet never have the feeling that you need or require anything. Since God's grace is your sufficiency, you do not live by effect alone, but by every word of truth that has been embodied in your consciousness, and by every passage of truth that you have made your own.

Affirming truths and denying errors will not make your demonstration. You must learn to live by every word of truth and make every word of truth a part of your consciousness so that it becomes flesh of your flesh, bone of your bone, until the past, present and future are all bound up in the conscious realization of God's grace as your sufficiency. In other words, your consciousness of truth is the source and substance and activity and law of your daily demonstration of good.

To those who are accepting the message of The Infinite Way as a way of life, I would like to sum this up by asking that you go back and bring your past into your present by spending some time during this next month consciously realizing that God's grace was your sufficiency in what you call your past; and that since before Abraham was, God's government of this universe has been so perfect that nothing of a discordant or inharmonious nature can happen to you or to anyone else, today or tomorrow. And so, should you hear of a sin, a disease, an accident, or a death, immediately realize that it could not have happened since, from the beginning of time, God has been the only law and reality unto His universe.

Then you will know the true meaning of spiritual healing. You will know what Christ-consciousness is; you will know what it means to live and move and have your being in God-consciousness, never accepting appearances, temptations, discords, sins, diseases, or accidents as anything other than temptations to believe in time and space.

If you are able to see that the past must become the present so that you are able to cover it all with the term *I am; I am* with you, *I am* with you in the past, *I am* with you in the present, *I am* with you since before Abraham was, *I am* is the law unto you, has been the law unto you, you will be able to take the next step and bring the future right down to the present, so that "unto the end of the world" will be embraced in your consciousness, the consciousness of the omnipresence of *I am*. In this way your whole universe will be embraced in the time and space since before Abraham was, unto the end of the world—all of it brought down to the here and now of *I am with you.*

The only time is God's time—*now.* God's time has existed since before Abraham was and will continue to exist until the end of the world. Because *I am* with you since before Abraham was and unto the end of the world, *I am* is the immediate present—*now.* God's grace, *now,* is your sufficiency, and the sufficiency unto your family and friends and students, and unto all who can accept God's grace.

Punishment

Sometimes secrets, so deep and so profound, are revealed to us that we are shaken from head to foot, and when this happens, we learn something not only new but something that must make a drastic change in our lives. Such is the experience when we realize the nature of punishment and the reasons for punishment in our experience.

To understand that God neither rewards nor punishes is an important step in your spiritual development. If you have been at all impressed with this statement, you have pondered and meditated upon it, and somewhere along this line of inner reflection, you have come to the realization that all of the religious theories which have been taught on the subject of punishment have been erroneous, and this itself should have made a startling change in your life. If you have the courage to continue your inner cogitation along this line, ultimately you will be led to the truth about punishment and the reason for punishment, and this will give you the opportunity to remold your life.

God is individual being, which means that God is the only Self, and there is no way for any hurt or evil to enter to defile the infinite purity of the Soul of God, nor anything at which evil can strike or attach itself. God is the Self of you, therefore God is the Self of me, and if I were in any way to hurt or offend you, to whom is my offense directed but to myself? This clarifies the Master's words: "Inasmuch as ye have done it unto one of the least of these my brethren, ye have done it unto me." With this understanding, you begin to see that every bit of good done by you at any time in your entire life has been a good done to, for, and within yourself; and you also begin to see that every evil or thought of evil you have ever directed toward another, every lie and evasion of truth, has been directed toward your own self, and therefore the punishment is inflicted upon you by you, because your act or thought of deceit, supposedly directed toward another, was actually directed toward yourself.

When the Master repeated the age-old wisdom: "Wherefore all things whatsoever ye would that men should do to you, do ye even so to them: for this is the law and the prophets;" he was giving us a principle: unless we do unto others as we would have others do unto us, we injure not the others but ourselves. In this present state of human consciousness, it is true that the evil thoughts and dishonest acts and thoughtless words that we send out to others do harm them temporarily, but in the end always it will be found that the injury was not nearly so much to them as it was to ourselves.

In the days to come, when men recognize the great truth that God is the Selfhood of each individual, the evil aimed at us from another will never touch us, but will immediately rebound upon the one who sends it. In the degree that we recognize God as our individual being, we also realize that no weapon that is formed against us can prosper, since the only "I," the only "Me," is God, and we will not fear what man can do to us, since the Selfhood of us is God and cannot be harmed, and our realization of this will quickly send back the evil, and much more quickly than has heretofore been the case.

Once the first realization of this truth comes to us, we understand that there is no longer any use concerning ourselves with what our neighbor does unto us, but looming large in our consciousness will be the realization that we must watch ourselves; morning, noon and night we must watch our thoughts, our words, our actions, to see that we ourselves do not send out anything of a negative nature which would be bound to have its result within our own being.

Never for a moment believe that this will result in your being good in order to avoid punishment. This revelation goes far deeper than that: it enables you to see that God is your Selfhood, and that anything of an erroneous or negative nature that emanates from any individual is given power only in the degree that you yourself give it power. In your meditation, it will result in the revelation of the nature of your true being—of God as the nature of your life and soul—and in that realization, you will see that this is the truth of all men, and that the only way and mode of successful living is to understand your neighbor to be yourself.

And so it is that whatever of good or of evil you do unto others, you do unto the Christ of your own being: "Inasmuch as ye have done it unto one of the least of these my brethren, ye have done it unto me."

Why?

When help is asked on certain physical or mental conditions, the question is often asked: Why is the so-called spiritual healing only a partial healing, and why sometimes is it never a complete healing? Also, why is it that a person about to undergo surgery asks for help and receives a miraculous healing, although not one that precludes the necessity for surgery? Why is it that the patient undergoing surgery is kept entirely free of infection or after-effect and makes a more rapid recovery than would normally be the case, and yet, if God has anything to do with that much of the healing, why did not God make the surgery unnecessary?

First of all, you must understand that there are no degrees of Truth. Truth is absolute. God is absolute. God is absolute Truth; God is absolute Being; God is infinite, eternal, immortal, omnipresent perfection. God is all. Therefore, the allness in the infinity and completeness and perfection of God being established, any measure less than that, experienced by the patient, represents the conditioned state of consciousness which makes it impossible to bring through or realize the completeness of the activity of God.

Here you have two factors: the consciousness of the practitioner and the consciousness of the patient. Let us assume that the consciousness of the practitioner is far higher and deeper than that of the patient, and so the patient comes to the practitioner with a conditioned state of consciousness in which it is not possible for him to open his consciousness completely to the fullness of the activity of God. It may be that there is so much attachment to the body and to the sense of personal health that the patient does not completely let go and thus receive the full benefit of the infinite completeness and perfection of the activity of God as individual consciousness. Although the practitioner may be an instrument for a complete and perfect healing, the conditioned consciousness of the patient does not always allow this to come through.

On the other hand, the practitioner may not be up to the experience of the miracle of complete healing. To be in the highest state of consciousness, the practitioner has reached that elevation of spiritual awareness in which no effort is ever made to contact God for the purpose of healing. He is abiding in the consciousness of God as individual being, hence in the realization that the individual is already at the standpoint of immortality and eternality, that state of being to which nothing can be added.

The practitioner who is trying to use truth over error, who is contacting God for the purpose of establishing harmony, or who is still in the third dimension of life, in which body is something separate and apart from spiritual consciousness, will make the mistake of being concerned with health as against disease, or will permit himself to be concerned with what appears to be something less than perfection in the visible scene.

For perfect healing the practitioner must abide in the consciousness of God as the infinite All, which means abiding in the fourth dimension of life in which no recognition is given to the pairs of opposites—good and evil, rich and poor, moral and immoral, immortal and mortal. In this fourth-dimensional consciousness or Christ-consciousness, the practitioner is never aware of someone or something to be healed or corrected but is always aware of the omnipresence of God's being.

When the practitioner is able to abide in Christ-consciousness and always have "that mind which was also in Christ Jesus," then the fullness of God's being freely flows, and regardless of whether it is an acute illness or a chronic one or whether the illness is at the point of surgery, the practitioner can bring to conscious realization and demonstration the complete healing or unfoldment of divine harmony. When the practitioner's consciousness is at all conditioned, then the healing can only come through in proportion to the degree of conditioning of the practitioner's consciousness. In order to complete the experience of instantaneous or complete healing, the patient also must approach this work without the conditioned thought of believing that the power of God can bring one through illness, even though not able to perform the entire unfoldment of harmony without the aid of surgery. At least, the patient should be able to relax with no preconceived thought or opinion as to what will take place and let the divine consciousness of the practitioner have full sway.

You can readily see that the main responsibility rests with the practitioner. When the practitioner truly rises above the pairs of opposites to that state of consciousness in which all sense of both health and disease are absent, and when any phase of the human picture does not bring a reaction which has behind it the desire to heal, correct, save, renew or regenerate, then in that spiritually illumined state of consciousness the practitioner will bring through greater works.

As you approach that state of non-reaction to the world of appearances whereby you do not react happily to the good appearances and certainly do not react fearfully or doubtfully to the evil appearances, you will do far greater healing works and will be able to impart to those who come to you a greater confidence in the great truth that God *is*, which means that harmony *is*, perfection *is*, reality *is*—and, in spite of all appearances to the contrary, good alone *is*.

IV

CONTEMPLATION DEVELOPS THE BEHOLDER

M ANY TIMES, THE young student is likely to believe that the spiritual or contemplative way of life is a life without discipline, but the very opposite of this is true because there is no life that requires greater discipline than does the spiritual life.

Life, as it is lived by most persons, is more or less undisciplined because little or no attempt is made by the individual to control the nature of his thinking. He is prone to accept everything that he sees or hears, usually rejoicing over what he thinks is good and moaning over what he believes to be evil, so that seldom does anyone ask himself, "Is this as good as it appears to be?" or, "Is this as evil as it appears to be?" Rather are appearances accepted in accordance with human judgment. In the spiritual way of life, however, that cannot be done because the entire spiritual life is based on the rejection of appearances.

Judge Not After Appearances

Commonly accepted metaphysics today teaches the rejection and denial of the appearance of evil and the realization of its unreal nature. But in the truly spiritual life, we have to go beyond merely rejecting evil as error because we also have to deny reality to that which appears as good; we have to unsee the humanly good appearances to the same degree that we unsee the humanly evil ones. Spiritually discerned, there is neither good nor evil, and it is on this premise that the entire spiritual universe is built. The discipline on this path lies in rejecting every appearance, whether it is good or evil, in the realization that whatever it is that is of God is invisible to the human senses.

"Why callest thou me good? there is none good but one, that is, God. … Neither do I condemn thee." In other words, there is no sitting in judgment on what appears to be evil, but neither is there any acceptance of the appearance of good: there is a recognition that the only real is the Invisible—the spiritual—and that is something that cannot be seen with the eyes, nor heard with the ears.

Under the old metaphysics, if we were confronted with an appearance and judged it to be evil, we immediately had to resist it: overcome, destroy, or remove it. If, on the other hand, we were confronted with an appearance of human good, we accepted it and rejoiced over it. The danger in this procedure, however, is that the very thing that appears to be good may, in and of itself, be evil or may change to evil, or its effect upon one may be of an evil nature.

A very good illustration of this is that nearly everybody would agree that having a million dollars—earning or inheriting it—is good, and yet the acquisition of a million dollars has proved to be the ruination of many persons. It has changed their nature and made them grasping because when some persons who have had little or nothing, and who have always been free and joyous in sharing that little, acquire more than they have been accustomed to having, many of them begin to hoard and grasp it and lay it up for a rainy day, fearing to spend it, so that what would appear to have been good has turned out to be evil for them.

In the human picture, practically everyone, almost without exception, rejoices at a birth and sorrows at a death. Nevertheless, more trouble has been caused in the world by birth than ever has been caused by death. So, if we were to judge from human appearances, we would be struck by the tragedies that take place as a result of birth, despite all the rejoicing, and by the uselessness and futility of much of the sorrowing at death.

These are extreme illustrations of how unwise it is to judge good or evil. Spiritually, however, judging as to good or evil goes far beyond being unwise. In a spiritual sense, it is absolutely wrong because there is a Power that is within each and every one of us, and this Power has as Its function the creating, maintaining, and sustaining of harmony in our existence, and when for any reason harmony is apparently taken from our lives, Its function is to restore it.

Living as a Witness
to the Activity of God

This Power or Principle is illustrated fully in the experience of Jesus Christ as narrated in the four Gospels. Jesus clearly revealed that his function was to heal the sick, raise the dead, feed the hungry, and forgive the sinner. Always he said, "I can of mine own self do nothing. ... the Father that dwelleth in me, he doeth the works." He always bore witness to the presence of God. In every one of the miracles performed by the Master, there was the denial of self and the glorification of the Father. Always it was, "I of my own self am doing nothing, for I of my own self am nothing. If I speak of myself, I bear witness to a lie. Therefore, it is not I who am good, it is not I who do the healing: I am but bearing witness to the presence and power of God."

How can we bear witness to this Power except by being still? If we do otherwise, we can no longer say that we are doing nothing or that we are nothing. We have become something the moment we do something. Therefore, when we are confronted with appearances—whether the appearance is called good or evil—we are being confronted with a human appearance, and if we would bear witness to the presence of God, we must do nothing, we must think nothing, and we must have no judgment. I am sure that you will not confuse this with an ignoring of our life's work, nor as a lazy do-nothing attitude, but you will understand this to be a disciplined withholding of judging as to good or evil and an attitude of expectancy—as of listening within. Be sure that you understand the significance of this attitude.

In order to make ourselves nothing, we must immediately realize within ourselves, "There is neither good nor evil: there is only God." Then, as we look out at the erroneous appearance with no judgment, there truly is neither good nor evil: there is only the presence of God, and now the Father within can perform Its function, and Its function is to dissolve the appearance and reveal God's glory—reveal Its own being.

Even though, to our sense, a healing appears, it is not really a healing: it is the dissolving of the material picture and the bringing to visibility of the spiritual one. There is only one way in which that can be done, and that is to withhold judgment as to good or evil, and then let the Father within do the work. Then, and then only, can we truthfully feel that we have had nothing to do with the demonstration except to bear witness to God in action.

This reminds me of a woman who was healed of a disease that had been pronounced incurable, and her husband, out of deep gratitude, went to the practitioner and offered him a check as a token of appreciation. When he began to express his gratitude, the practitioner said, "Oh, I didn't do it—God did it," at which the man put the check back in his pocket and replied, "Oh, well, then I don't owe you anything. I'll give the check to God."

As a matter of fact, insofar as the healing was concerned, the practitioner was right, but the husband was also right. The practitioner had not brought about the healing: he had merely borne witness to God in action, so therefore there was no money due because of the healing. Where the husband was wrong was that he should have known that if the practitioner had not been available and had not been able to bear witness to God's grace, there would have been no healing. If the practitioner had been dependent for his livelihood on hanging telephone wires, tending furnaces, or whatever else his job might have been, he perhaps might not have been able to live in the Spirit and to bear witness to God when called upon. Giving him money, therefore, was not for the healing. It was merely to enable him to be free of other obligations so that he could keep his consciousness clear and free of entanglements and could always be in the Spirit to bear witness to Its activity.

When you witness healing works, always remember what it is you are witnessing. You are not witnessing the power of an individual, for an individual has no such power: you are merely witnessing an individual who is keeping himself free of the appearance-world and maintaining himself in a consciousness of no judgment, so that the grace of God can come through, because the grace of God cannot come through the human mind. And what is the human mind but anybody's mind that is still indoctrinated with the belief in two powers?

Discipline in the Contemplative Life

Regardless of how much knowledge of truth a person may have, no matter how many years he may have studied truth, he may still have no healing power. It is not how many statements of truth a person knows intellectually or can declare. Healing power has to do with the degree of the actual awareness and conviction attained of the nonpower of appearances. It is for this reason that the spiritual path is a path of discipline, and every disciple or student must begin at some moment in his career to withhold judgment.

In proportion as this consciousness of no judgment is attained, the appearances in this world automatically change as they touch your consciousness. This is because your consciousness is not reacting to good or to evil and is, therefore, able to pierce the veil of illusion, even the veil of good illusion, and see that there is nothing to fear and nothing to gloat about because what you are seeing is not the spiritual creation, but a finite concept of it: sometimes good and sometimes bad, sometimes rich and sometimes poor, sometimes healthy and sometimes sick, sometimes alive and sometimes dead. But none of that is true of God's kingdom.

The Master's statement, "My kingdom is not of this world," helps us to discipline ourselves. Instantly, we shut out everything that we see or hear, realizing that that is "this world," but it is not *My* kingdom, the Christ-kingdom, the spiritual kingdom; and therefore, we neither love, hate, nor fear it. Think of the discipline involved in refraining from all attempts to change the appearance when we are in the midst of what seems to be a problem for ourselves or another. Think, think of any discordant appearance that you have ever seen, heard, tasted, touched, or smelled; see the discipline that is necessary to refrain from attempting to alter, change, or do something about it; and then be convinced and know, "My kingdom—the place where I live, move, and have my being—is not of this world. Therefore, I have nothing to do about this world except to know that it is not of *My* kingdom."

As we withdraw judgment—which means to withdraw our hate, fear, or love of the appearance—it is then that this Invisible, the Spirit of God, which is in us, can immediately go to work to change the appearance.

Self-Preservation Is the Dominant Note in Human Experience

When the disciples were afraid because of the storm at sea, they awakened the Master, but he did not attempt to stop the storm by praying to God because he knew that he was being faced with an illusory appearance. He merely "rebuked the wind, and said unto the sea, Peace, be still. And the wind ceased, and there was a great calm." What the disciples were seeing was something more than a storm: they were probably not aware of it, but they were seeing a selfhood apart from God, and above all they may have been afraid that they were going to lose their lives.

The disciples, seized as they were by fear, were responding as most people do to that first law of nature, the law of self-preservation. In the human picture, that law (if we can dignify it by the name of law) is responsible for most of the evil that is in the world. A person would not steal if it were not that he is trying to preserve his personal and human sense of life. He is hoping to keep himself from starving or from being a failure, and he is staving off lack and limitation. In short, he is preserving his own human sense of identity.

What but self-preservation lies behind every war? Men call it patriotism because they claim that wars are fought to preserve the nation, but a nation is only a group of individuals, so in the final analysis it is the preservation and perpetuation of themselves, of their human lives, and human supply that induces them to enter into a war. However, the horror is that people are always willing to sacrifice and send their children off to get killed as long as they can stay home and be saved. Children are not as important to most people as they themselves are. The children must go off and get killed or wounded or demented so that others can stay home and have abundance.

In the storm, then, the disciples were not really afraid of the storm. What difference would a storm have made to them if they had not believed that their lives were in danger? Who cares whether the wind is forty or a hundred miles an hour if there is no danger to one's life or limb? It is only while there is fear of the loss of life that anybody cares whether the storm rages or ceases.

Many of us would be able to attain our release from the world of cause and effect, that is, from the world of appearances, if only we could bring to bear upon the situation that great assurance of the Master, "It is I; be not afraid." To know this truth would immediately divest us of any judgment as to the nature of the appearance.

"It is I; be not afraid"—I, *God, is the only Life; I, God, is the life of individual being, and that Life cannot be lost and It cannot be destroyed. Let the storm do what it will. I cannot fear.*

Similarly, who cares how many germs there are in the world unless we can be made to believe that germs can destroy our life? Ah! That sets up an antagonism in us, and we are going out now to wipe all the germs off the face of the earth. Why? What have we against germs? Nothing. Except that they threaten destruction to our own lives or our own health.

But suppose we came to the realization that our life is indestructible, that neither life nor death can separate us from God? Now what difference would germs make? And in that realization, the battle against error—that particular form of error—would cease, and none of these things would move us:

"None of these things move me." My life is God; my life is in God; my life is with God; and neither life nor death can separate me from God.

In that realization, death itself no longer has any fears or terrors. No one can possibly fear death once he realizes that neither death nor life can separate him from the Life that he is, the Life that is his being.

The Detachment of a Beholder

If we accept the Master's statement, "My kingdom is not of this world," we do not have to fight, remove, or overcome anything in the external world:

"It is I; be not afraid." I am the life of you; I, God, the Spirit of God in you is your life, your being, and the substance of your body.

When we are no longer afraid of anything in the external world, then we automatically arrive at a state of consciousness that no longer concerns itself with the good appearances or fears the evil appearances, but looks out at them with a sense of detachment as an onlooker or a beholder, with no interest in changing, improving, or destroying them: with just the attitude of a beholder.

In this attitude of a beholder, our personal mental powers come to a stop, and it is as if we were watching a sunrise or a sunset. Nobody in his right mind believes that he can hasten the rising of the sun or its setting, or that he can increase its beauty. Therefore, in watching a sunrise or a sunset, we become completely the beholder, watching nature at work, watching God at work. We never enter into the picture, never seek to change, remove, destroy, or attempt to improve it in any way. As a beholder, we are always in the absolute center of our own being; and as a beholder, we can truthfully say, "What a beautiful sunset," or, "What a beautiful sunrise God is bringing about."

If we were in an art gallery, standing before the works of the great masters, we would be beholders because all that we would be trying to do would be to draw from the picture what the artist had placed there. We do not try to improve the picture; we do not try to destroy it; all that we seek to do is to draw forth from the picture what the artist has created and placed there for our enjoyment. We do not enter the picture: we behold it. If we enter anything, it would be the consciousness of the artist to behold exactly what he beheld because we are now of one consciousness—one mind.

When we hear a symphony, we do not enter the symphony: We stand off as a beholder, this time listening, listening to what the composer had in mind. We are not trying to improve his work, nor are we trying to destroy it; we are merely trying to understand it. Even if it sounds like bad music to us—unpleasant, discordant, or offbeat—we still do not try to change it: We stand still, without judgment, trying to grasp what the composer had in mind, and it would not be surprising if eventually, we found ourselves right inside the consciousness of that composer, hearing the music as he heard it when he put it on paper. Then we would have the same understanding of it that he had.

So it is that God created this universe and all that is therein, and it is good. To our finite sense, however, we see some of this universe as evil and some of it as good, and strangely enough, the man right beside us may be seeing what we call good as evil; what we see as evil, he may be seeing as good; so therefore, we cannot be seeing this universe the way God made it. We are seeing it through our ignorance of God, our lack of God-awareness, just as we might see a painting or hear music and, because of our ignorance, be unable to discern what the artist or the composer had in mind.

As we look out at this world of appearances without judgment, it is as if we were realizing that God's spirit made all that is and made it spiritual, and in that realization we now behold a spiritual universe, even though at the moment we do not understand or see it the way the grand architect of the universe created it. We cannot see through the eyes of Him who designed and formed this universe while we are looking out of human eyes, but by looking at this world without judgment, it is as if we were trying to see what God created, as God sees it, in other words, entering into the consciousness of God.

The only way we can do that is to withhold judgment and be still, seeing neither good nor evil, being a beholder, and letting the Father present the picture to us. We just bear witness; we just behold—but not with the idea of healing anyone, not with the idea of improving or enriching anyone—merely with the idea of beholding the picture as God made it and as God sees it.

Withhold Judgment as to Good or Evil

The only way that the mind of God can be consciously expressed through us is when we are withholding human judgment as to good or evil and letting ourselves be beholders, and then the Spirit of God lives in and through us, changing the picture from what it seems to be, and revealing to us that which was always there, even though finite sense could not discern it.

Flowers, beautiful and colorful as they are, actually have no color. We are not seeing the flowers as they are because color does not exist. There are light waves, and when they strike our eyes, we interpret the rate of their vibration as color. A certain vibration is interpreted as red, another as purple, and another as blue. It is color only when it touches our eyesight, and if our eyesight is not accurate, we may see one color as red, whereas another person may see it as quite a different color.

It is the same with sound. If, in a forest, the largest tree were to topple over, there would never be a sound heard in that forest because no sound is taking place. There are invisible sound waves set up by the falling tree, but the silence is absolute and complete until it touches an eardrum. Those sound waves must touch an eardrum before there can be any sound, and if they touched an impaired eardrum, there would still be no sound, no matter how loud the sound might seem to be to you.

We are always judging by the limitation of our finite senses. We are not seeing this world as it is; we are seeing this world as our mind interprets it. In some parts of the world, people go about naked, and in that kind of a civilization nobody thinks there is anything wrong about it. The fact is that being clothed or unclothed is a concept of life that has evolved, not life itself. The Father said, "Who told thee that thou wast naked?"

As we live the life of contemplation, therefore, we find ourselves gradually withdrawing judgment from appearances, and when we see, or when we are told about erroneous appearances, we do not react to them, and they do not register in our consciousness and as far as they are concerned, our mind is a blank. We have no desire to change, alter, or improve the appearance presented to us: we are just beholders waiting for God to reveal it to us as it is.

"Awake Thou That Sleepest"

"I shall be satisfied, when I awake, with thy likeness." A spiritually awakened person is completely satisfied with the people of this world because he knows them as they really are, and even though he sees the discords and problems that they are experiencing, he also knows that these are no part of their real being, but only a part of that educated sense which is trying to preserve an already immortal life, or trying to get more supply for one who is, and always has been, joint-heir with Christ in God. Therefore, he looks with compassion on those whom he knows are in ignorance of their true identity or those who do not understand the nature of God's world.

Suppose you come to the realization that "I and my Father are one," that the life of God is your individual life and therefore your life is indestructible, and that neither life nor death can ever separate you from God, which is life eternal and immortal. Now you begin to lose your fear of death, you begin to lose your fear of the burglar with a gun in his hand because you know that you have no life to lose. No longer do you fear for your life. Your life is now recognized as God—indestructible, immortal, and eternal. Death? Even death cannot separate you from God.

"Awake thou that sleepest," and learn that God is your life. Neither life nor death can take your life from you. Life goes on whether you live in the East or the West; it goes on whether you live in this house or that house; it goes on whether you are young or old or even whether you have gone into the realm beyond. Life is a continuous experience because life is God, and God is life.

The Contemplative Life Brings a Consciousness of Life as Indestructible

Through the contemplative life, you come to a whole new state of consciousness in which, while you are still aware that there are evils in the world, no longer do you sit in judgment on them or condemn them, no longer do you misunderstand them. Now you have compassion because you understand why they are taking place. Furthermore, you know that they must continue to take place in each person's experience until he is awakened.

When an individual is awakened to the fact that life is indestructible, immortal, and eternal, he cannot fear death; and once he no longer fears death, he cannot know death. No one can experience anything that is not a part of his consciousness, and when death is no longer a part of consciousness, he cannot die.

Leave this scene? Yes! Yes! That is like a bouquet of flowers. In a few days the form of the flowers will perish, but not their life. The life will go on and be manifested in other forms of the same kind of flowers, and it will be the same life. It will not be a different life. The life that is in a bouquet of roses today or the life that was in roses ten thousand years ago is the same life.

Your life and your identity and your consciousness will still be here ten thousand years from now, but in a different form. You will not be gone: only your form will change. That this is true is evidenced by the fact that when you came into this world, you weighed six, seven, eight, nine, or ten pounds, but that form has been changing ever since. Even the form of the organs of the body has changed. Organs not developed when we were born have developed and matured, and some of these at a certain age stop functioning, but we go on just the same: there is no change in us. We are the same person, the same life, the same consciousness, despite the changes that take place in our bodies. The child-body is not that of the adult-body, and the body of the aged is not the same as the body of the adult; but the individual is the same, the life is the same, the soul is the same, the consciousness is the same. Only the outer form changes.

So it will be that, unless I am lifted out of this life, I will be here a thousand years from now, even though the form may be different. As a matter of fact, the sex could be different, and the reason is that *I*—and this applies to every one of us—*I* has no sex. Once you become aware of the *I* that you are, you will find It completely independent of body and completely independent of sex, manifesting as either sex, even though it will still be *I*. That is because *I* is spiritual; *I* is one with God; *I* is of the nature of God. Therefore, *I* is without finite form, yet *I* can manifest as, in, or through finite form. When you have realized that, the sting of death leaves you because you will know then that you are *I*, and *I* will always be your state of consciousness, except that you will progressively elevate until there is nothing finite left.

That *I* is the secret of the transcendental life. With the realization, "It is I; be not afraid," and that that *I* is God, all fear goes, all judgment, all condemnation, and then even as you look out upon the world and witness the discords that hold mankind in bondage, the feeling is there: "Just think, if the people of this world could awaken to their true identity!" And that is all there is to it. They are not evil; they are not bad: They are just fulfilling the law of self-preservation, and so we do not sit in judgment on them because we have done the same thing.

"It Is I; Be Not Afraid"

When we throw a bomb at somebody else—an atomic bomb or a bomb of hatred or gossip—or if we kill in self-defense, we are doing just what the world is doing: we are operating from the standpoint of the law of self-preservation, and the self we are trying to preserve is a finite sense of self that has no contact with God. That is why we are trying to save it. If we understood our true identity as one with God, we would not have to try to save it. God can govern and care for His own universe.

In the face of danger, we withdraw judgment and realize, "Whatever is real is God-maintained and God-sustained. Whatever is real is of God, and it is permanent and eternal. I do not have to lift my finger to save it, to preserve it, or to do anything about it. I merely have to behold God in action." We must sit, not in judgment but completely without judgment, in the realization that this is God's universe.

"It is I; be not afraid. ... My kingdom is not of this world"—My kingdom is intact. All that God has joined together, no man can put asunder. My Father's life and my life are one; therefore my life cannot be put asunder by sin, by disease, by lack, by death,

by war, or by any other means. Nothing can put asunder my life, because my life is joined to God's life: it is one with God: God maintains my life eternally, immortally, and neither life nor death can separate life from itself or change that relationship.

In the face of danger of any nature, we stand by without judgment and bear witness to God. Then afterward, when the harmony has been restored and safety and security realized, we can repeat with the Master, "I of my own self did nothing. The Father within me did the work." Now, of course, there was one thing we did that was very important and very difficult, and that was to come to the place of being a beholder. The discipline of the spiritual path consists of the ability to discipline one's self so as not to see a picture that has to be changed, altered, improved, or removed, and the vision to look out at the pictures this world presents with this conviction, "It is I; be not afraid," and then stand still and bear witness while God brings about the transformation of the visible scene.

"It is I; be not afraid. … My kingdom is not of this world. … Cease ye from man, whose breath is in his nostrils: for wherein is he to be accounted of?" These are the three scriptural passages that have been the foundation of my healing work ever since the early 1930's. Before that, I was doing healing work, but without knowing why or how, or what the principle was. It was, you might say, just a gift of God. But in the early 1930's, I was given the revelation of those three statements.

"Cease ye from man, whose breath is in his nostrils: for wherein is he to be accounted of?" Do not try to change man, improve him, or heal him, and certainly do not judge or condemn him: take no account of him. In other words, be still!

Then came, "My kingdom is not of this world." Therefore, do not judge by the appearance of this world, because in *My* kingdom, harmony is. *My* kingdom is a spiritual kingdom, and heaven is established even on earth as it is in heaven. Again, you cease from all attempts to change, improve, heal, or reform.

The secret of the success that I have had in my work in prisons is in going to the prison without any desire to reform anybody, not blinding myself to the fact that humanly, these men and women were not living up to a spiritual standard, but realizing that whatever they had done had been done because of the urgency of the law of self-preservation, because of ignorance of their true identity. Therefore, there was no more condemnation for them than a schoolteacher has for a student who comes to learn. He knows in advance that his student does not know what he is going to learn from the teacher, but he does not condemn the student for that. He recognizes that the student is ignorant and he is going to change that ignorance by imparting knowledge.

So it is that when I have gone into prisons, I have not condemned or judged: I have realized, "Here are people in ignorance of the fact that God is their life and that they do not have to sustain it. God is their supply, and they do not have to get supply. They are joint-heirs with Christ in God." So my work has been to enlighten them as to their true identity because once they know that, their whole nature will be changed.

As human beings, there is not one of us without sin, whether in the act of commission or in the act of desiring. We are transformed in only one way: by coming into the awareness of our true identity, and then learning to be still and knowing that "I am God," and that because *I* is God, that *I* governs Its own universe; It maintains it, and It sustains it. In fact, that *I* is the bread and the meat and the wine and the water unto Its creation; and therefore, each one of us has *I*, each one of us has in the midst of him, closer than breathing, that which the Master says is the mission of the Father within, that which heals, saves, redeems, resurrects, and feeds. That *I*, each one of us has, and It is the Christ. In the awareness of that *I*, we become beholders of the Christ in action, and as beholders of the Christ in action, we are able to pierce the veil of illusion, and then instead of seeing the ugly picture that the human mind has drawn, we begin to see reality.

Across the Desk

Today, world news holds the spotlight wherever one travels, and wherever there is world news, there is fear and anxiety. The past centuries in which this world has lived without spiritual intercession have made men lose their hope that God can save, but the century that has brought forth great spiritual healing ministries will also reveal the nature and activity of spiritual power in the wider affairs of mankind.

In the minds of most persons concerned with the major problems of the world today, as always, the great desire is for victory. Capitalism seeks a victory over communism and vice versa; trade unions want more and greater victories over the very source of their incomes, while on the other hand there are still some unenlightened capitalists with dreams of victories over labor.

Neither the Republican Party nor the Democratic Party, Labor or Conservative, Socialist or Liberal wants the peace and prosperity of nations but rather victory over each other.

Who but the blind can believe that the United States, England, and France, and their allies won the First and Second World Wars? Look over the list of all of them, and ask, "What price victory?" And yet the lifeblood and wealth of all nations continue to be spent in seeking still another victory. But to turn now to spiritual power for victory would be to revert to the pagan teachings of the pre-Christian era.

Does your vision open to a greater scene than victorious armies marching into civilians' homes and hospitals? Can you envision something better than medals for mass slaughter? Will your vision carry you to greater heights than the alternatives of one kind of material force as against another?

Withdraw your gaze from the picture that materialism would paint for you; turn within and see what promise you find as your gaze travels from the scene without to the kingdom within. What vision do you see when the word "victory" is dropped from thought?

When victory is no longer your goal, spiritual power will reveal itself to you.

V

THE RELATIONSHIP OF ONENESS

YOUR WORLD AND mine is an outpicturing of our consciousness: When that consciousness is imbued with truth, our universe expresses harmony, orderliness, prosperity, joy, peace, power, and dominion; when there is an absence of truth in our consciousness—an acceptance of world values and world beliefs—then our world takes on the complexion of the chance, change, and luck characteristic of world belief. All conditions reflect the activity of the consciousness of the individuals concerned.

Your world is embodied in your consciousness; it reflects the state of your consciousness because your consciousness governs your world. Your awareness of truth is the law unto your world, but on the other hand, your ignorance of truth likewise becomes a law unto it. For example, there is no law of darkness because you know that darkness can be dispelled by the presence of light. Yet in the absence of light, darkness would claim presence; and just so, in the absence of truth in your consciousness, ignorance, lies, appearances, discords, and inharmony claim to be present. Therefore, in the absence of the activity of truth in your consciousness, your world will reflect chance, luck, human belief, medical belief, or astrological belief; but the activity of truth operating in and as your consciousness becomes a law of harmony unto everything in your world and makes everything concerning you reflect the harmony of your consciousness.

Suppose that you find yourself in a situation where you are faced with a roomful of people with whom you must work in some capacity or other—talk to them, instruct them, or serve them. As you look at them, they present a variety of appearances—good people, bad, sick, well, rich, and poor. How can you establish a sense of oneness with all these people? To feel a sense of union with any other person means, first of all, that you must make your contact with the Spirit within and find your own completeness; you must make your contact with the Father within, whereupon you automatically become one with every other individual within range of your consciousness.

This is your opportunity to apply the principles of The Infinite Way. Look over or through every person in the room to God:

God is the animating principle of every individual; God is the mind of every person here, the intelligence expressing as person. God is the only love, and God being infinite, God is all love; therefore, God is the love of individual being, and being filled with the love which is God, no individual can be used as an instrument for hate, envy, jealousy, or malice.

Realization such as that will lift you above personalities into the realm of pure being.

You may be confronted with evidences of misunderstanding, but what difference does it make what the appearance is? Right where that appearance is foisting itself upon your mind, God is. You are dealing only with God, not with beliefs, persons, or conditions.

Over and over again, it has been proved that when confronting people who have fallen prey to anger or when meeting with vicious animals poised and ready to attack, by merely holding to the realization of God as the real entity or

identity—the real being—God as the only law, the only substance, the only cause, the only effect, what we call healing
takes place. This method of treatment never leaves the realm
of God, never comes down to the level of man or person or
condition or circumstance, nor does it take unemployment,
sin, or disease into consideration.

It is so easy to say that this is good and that is evil, this
is of God and that is of the devil, but it is when a person or
circumstance claims to have the power to crucify or set you
free, to cause you trouble, to do this or that to you, that you
must take your stand and realize:

*My being is in Christ, and as long as I maintain my being
in Christ, only the Christ can operate in my consciousness—
which is the one consciousness, the consciousness of every person
in the world.*

In other words, when you look out at this world and
see persons or circumstances claiming to have power over
you for good or evil, you again must acknowledge that your
being is in Christ and only the Christ-inspired can have any
influence in your affairs.

Several years ago, in a period of distress, it came to me
that I must love those who hate me, I must give love for
ingratitude, and my answer was, "Father, I just can't do it. I
don't know how to do it. Yes, I can be a hypocrite and say that
I love these people who are hating, condemning, judging,
and fighting me, but I can tell you truthfully that I don't—I
don't know how to love them. It is true I have no antagonism
toward them because I know what motivates them and I do
not blame them. If I did not have a little understanding of
Your infinite love, I might do the same thing in their position;
so I have no sense of judgment or criticism or condemnation

of them. I can even say, 'Father, forgive them; for they know not what they do'—but to love them! No, I cannot honestly say that I love them. I just cannot do that. If there is to be any loving, I am perfectly willing to be the avenue through which You, God, can love them through me. If that can be arranged, let's have it that way, but don't ask me to love them because that is beyond my capacity."

It was less than a minute after that that I settled down into a beautiful peace, went to sleep, and awakened completely healed. It is impossible to love ingratitude, injustice, misrepresentation, and lies, but we can be willing to let God take over: "God, You who could love the thief on the cross and the woman taken in adultery, You love these people, too."

What was required for the demonstration that I had to make? Was it not the ability to "nothingize" myself, even to the extent of not trying to be self-righteous about loving my enemy? When you say that you are loving your enemy, that is self-righteousness. We have to learn to let God do the loving and be willing to be an instrument through which God's love flows to our friends and to our enemies.

In the world, there are good people and bad people, just and unjust people, but when you climb up into that circle of God, you find that God is the principle of all people; God is the only principle of people, the animating love and life and truth of all people—those in your business, in your social relationships, and in your home.

Your home is a composite of your consciousness of home. You are the doorkeeper of your household, and you should stand guard at the door to see that nothing gets past that door which does not have the right to be there. This door, however, is not a material door. The only door there is, is the door of consciousness, and the only door for which you are responsible is that door. What do you allow to get past your door, your consciousness? Do you accept contagion and infection as power in your home? Are you a party to discord and bickering? You should make it a matter of daily realization that nothing can enter the doorway of consciousness except the truth of being, and that no suggestion of human power, whether physical, material, or mental, is law. Any belief that enters your home must first enter through your consciousness, and the truth of being in your consciousness will act as a law of annihilation to any false belief that would intrude.

Everything that comes within range of your consciousness will take on the nature and character of that consciousness. Your own life is not only affected by what gets past the door of your consciousness, but the life of everyone who has brought himself to your consciousness is affected, and that includes the members of your family and sometimes the members of your community and church. All these look to you for bread; they look to you for the truth of being, but oftentimes your mind is so occupied with concern over your own discords and inharmonies that they are turned away without the divine substance which they sought from you.

Deep within every person is a hunger for the bread of life. Friends, relatives, and even acquaintances who find their way to your home ostensibly seeking companionship, supply, or any form of material good, even though from their point of view that may be their purpose, are in reality longing and craving for the true substance of life, the meat that perisheth not. If you give them money and give them that alone, if you give them your physical, human companionship, and give them that alone, you are giving them a stone: You are not giving them the bread of life; you are not lifting their state of consciousness. This you can do only in the degree that you are specifically entertaining the consciousness of truth within your being as they come to you:

God is the substance and the activity of my home; God is the consciousness of every individual who enters my home, whether it is family or friends. Nothing enters my home to contaminate or violate its sanctity, because God is my only home. As long as my home appears on earth as a material structure, it will express the harmony of God. Those in that home will either reflect that harmony or they will be removed because nothing unlike God can remain in my home—my temple, my being, my body. Anything of a discordant nature that would enter, or might temporarily be permitted to enter, will be removed in its time and in such a way that it will injure no one, but be a blessing to everyone involved.

Since God is my consciousness, nothing can enter that consciousness that "defileth or maketh a lie," and even if I, in my ignorance or human softness, permit something to enter which has no place there, it will not long remain. The consciousness of Truth and Life which I am will heal it or remove it. I am willing that everybody and everything that enters my consciousness shall be either healed or removed. I dare not cling to anyone and say, "With all your faults, I still need you and want you." I take my stand with God and, if necessary, leave father, mother, brother, sister, husband, or wife in order to dwell in the secret place of the most High.

Clinging to that which you know is not right just because of human emotion very often does much to impede your spiritual demonstration. Each one must rely upon inner guidance to determine when to let go of human ties and when not to let go.

Nearly every marriage ceremony contains some version of the statement, "that which God has joined together let no man put asunder." The truth is that what God has joined together, what God has brought together in oneness and unity, no man *can* put asunder. It would be an utter impossibility for man to have power over God and over God's work. No man has the power to undo the work of God. In the world of appearances, there can be temporary strife, discord and inharmony—and there will be, but not for you if you climb into that circle of God and there live in the constant realization that what God has made is forever, and what God has brought together no man can put asunder.

In dealing with a marital problem, you would realize that since God is One, the only relationship that exists is a relationship of oneness, and there can be no division or separation in that oneness—no inharmony or discord in One. The moment there are two, there can be any kind of discord and inharmony, but that is impossible in oneness.

Many people believe that a realization such as this would ensure a couple's remaining together, and that, therefore, no divorce or separation could possibly follow. Nothing could be further from the truth. A couple may be married and may be legally one, and yet they may not actually be one in their being—they may not be spiritually one. Therefore, this realization of oneness might bring about a separation or divorce much more quickly than would otherwise be the case, freeing both husband and wife from the yoke of inharmony and discord and enabling both to find their oneness elsewhere. No two people can realize oneness or true happiness when life resolves itself into a continuous battle of misunderstandings and disagreements. The marital relationship without love is a sin.

A practitioner of spiritual healing should never intrude into the family life of any person or of any couple, nor judge humanly as to whether two people should get married, remain married, be separated, or divorced. That is not the business of a spiritual healer, and, furthermore, there is no easy way of knowing from outward appearances what the truth of the situation is. In all cases of marital discord and inharmony, hold to the fact that God is the only one, and there is only one marriage, the mystical marriage. Such a marriage is God-ordained, and no man can rend it asunder.

Sometimes the very best way that God can maintain that oneness is by severing the human or legal tie. Never believe for a minute that just knowing oneness will keep all marriages together, because it will not. Knowing oneness will keep a person one with his good, and if that good means celibacy, marriage, separation, or divorce, that is what will happen. No one has the right to outline how a demonstration is to take place because everything must unfold in accordance with spiritual good, not in accordance with some human being's idea of what constitutes good. No one should set himself up as being competent to decide what is humanly good.

It is unwise to attempt to protect loved ones from discords and inharmonies which, knowingly or unknowingly, they have brought and are bringing upon themselves. It is better to give up anxious concern, loose them, and let them live with some of their discords, because the overprotection which would keep them from the results of their own conduct is often the stumbling block which prevents them from awakening to the truth of being. Their very suffering may be the needling necessary to awaken them. Each one of us has to learn the lesson of "loose him, and let him go." Loose your loved ones into Christ; loose them into God, and let the law of God govern.

Regardless of the amount of spiritual realization attained by some people and the measure of its practice in daily life, there are always those who for one reason or another cannot or will not respond. The greatest known witness to the spiritual life was the Master, Christ Jesus, and yet even he had his Judas, his doubting Thomas, his denying Peter, and his disciples who fell asleep in the garden. Undoubtedly, both Peter and Thomas awakened and atoned for their temporary lapse. Of Judas, there is no proof of any awakening to this spiritual light. Furthermore, there was a time when the spiritual impetus found no answer in Saul of Tarsus, and yet, at a certain given moment, he not only responded to it but he became a great living witness to it.

Therefore, no one need despair if those in his family, his church group, in his nation, or in the world at large are not responding at this moment to the spiritual impulse. In their own time they will. With some of them, it may take days, weeks, months, years, and with some it may take many lifetimes to come. But sooner or later, every knee will bend—every knee. At some time or other, all men will be taught of God.

People believe that they are held back because of the lack of demonstration of someone around them or that for one reason or another, the lack of demonstration on the part of someone else may have an adverse influence upon them. That could never be true unless they themselves permitted it. Each one is responsible for his own spiritual demonstration, and it is useless to blame the other fellow for a lack of spiritual courage.

No less an authority than the Master has taught that in order to attain the stature of Christhood, it is necessary to leave mother, father, brother, sister "for my sake." Why not face the fact that most people are not yet ready to leave those who they believe are acting in such a way as to hold back their demonstration? So no one should blame anyone—not even himself—but quickly realize that only the acceptance of a universal belief in a selfhood apart from God could hypnotize him into believing that any influence outside his own being could act upon him. How could anyone influence, help, or hinder another person's demonstration? How is it possible for anyone to come between him and his realization of Christhood? That can only be if there is a dependence on a human being.

If men and women accept the universal belief that their support and supply come from husband, wife, investments, or business, they have brought themselves under the law. Before people have any knowledge of spiritual wisdom, such a reliance is natural, but after they have learned the truth of their identity as being one with the Father, if they then persist in placing their "faith in princes"—their reliance on friends or family—instead of freeing themselves and living under grace, they will continue to live under the human law of limitation. In spiritual living, there is no dependence upon any person or thing: There is a sharing, but there is never dependence. Whatever is shared with another is shared from the infinite bounty of God:

"I and my Father are one": That is my relationship to God, and that is God's relationship to me. It has nothing to do with any person; It has nothing to do with relatives, friends, or associates. My good is in no way dependent on them, nor is their good dependent on me. My good is God's allness made manifest as my individual being.

When this oneness is glimpsed, every relationship becomes one of friendship, joy, and cooperation. If our dependence is not on others, then no lack or loss would be suffered if our relationships with others were wiped away because good is inherent in our relationship to God, and it does not lie within anyone's power to lose the relationship of joint-heir with Christ in God. The human picture does not testify to that because, in order to benefit by the relationship of Father and son, an activity of truth must take place in individual consciousness.

When you learn to "call no man on earth your father," automatically every man, woman, and child on this earth become your brother and sister. According to human testimony, you may be an only child and you may have no relatives on earth, but once you have agreed to "call no man on earth your father," that is no longer true because you have made a brother and sister of everybody in this universe. People who have looked upon you as a stranger suddenly feel, "I know this person; I feel as if I have always known him." Even though you are not blood-brothers or sisters, no barrier exists between you because now a higher relationship than that of blood-brother or sister has been established: Now you are brothers and sisters by divine ordinance.

There is a bond, a spiritual tie, which binds together all the children of God. This is not a tie to human beings or mortals, and that is why those who persist in remaining on the human or mortal level ultimately drift out of the experience of the more spiritually illumined. Each one draws unto himself those with whom he is spiritually united, his spiritual brothers and sisters, but those who live and insist on living on the mortal or material plane sooner or later drift away from him, and sometimes the greatest heartaches come from trying to hold on to them.

Along the way, you may meet with falsehood, deception, and vilification; sometimes your friends and relatives are asleep, not upholding you, sometimes even resisting or obstructing you. You must reach the point in your unfoldment where that is of no consequence to you. It makes no difference in your life who fails you: It makes a difference only to them because they have failed in their demonstration of their Christhood, but it will make no difference to you if you have learned your relationship to God.

Since God is the life, wisdom, activity, and supply of your being, you have no demonstration to make which is dependent upon anyone here on earth. You are spiritually fed, clothed, and housed. Your utter and complete reliance is on this truth that all that the Father has is yours. If the whole earth were wiped away, this one truth would remain, "I and my Father are one," and all that the Father has would still be yours.

When the Master taught his disciples to leave mother, brother, sister for his sake, he did not mean that they should leave those of their spiritual household. "Who is my mother, or my brethren? And he looked round about on them which sat about him, and said, Behold my mother and my brethren! For whosoever shall do the will of God, the same is my brother, and my sister, and mother." All who can meet together on a spiritual level of love are bound together from now until eternity, sharing forever with each other.

VI

INTRODUCTION

N O ONE IS going to pick up this book and read it unless it is someone who has already known quiet moments of inner reflection, someone who has been plagued by frustration, lack of success, or lack of harmony, and who has pondered long and seriously why life should be so unsatisfactory. Because this was my experience and because that experience led to the writing of this book, only those who have had a similar experience and have been goaded by that same unfathomable question will be interested in reading further to discover what I have found and how it has benefited me.

There have been many times in my life when I have had reason to be dissatisfied with the way life was going, dissatisfied to the point of quietly, inwardly wondering and pondering the possibility of finding a way out. Long periods of success and happiness, followed by dissatisfaction and unhappiness, finally led to longer and more frequent periods of introspection, cogitation, and contemplation of life and what it was all about. In one of these experiences, while I cannot say that I heard a voice, I do know that I received an impression that was something like an inner being saying to me, "Thou wilt keep him in perfect peace whose mind is stayed on thee." I must admit that this was a startling experience because up to this time, I had been almost totally unfamiliar with the Bible; it had not been a daily companion but merely a matter of occasional reading.

71

Later, more thoughts of this same nature unfolded, and I began to realize that throughout Scripture, we are told to "lean not unto thine own understanding. In all thy ways acknowledge him, and he shall direct thy paths. ... He that dwelleth in the secret place of the most High shall abide under the shadow of the Almighty. ... in quietness and in confidence shall be your strength." As passage after passage unfolded and revealed itself, I was led ultimately to that grandest experience of all, in which the great Master, Christ Jesus, reveals that if we abide in the Word and let the Word abide in us, we shall bear fruit richly, and that actually it is God's pleasure that we prosper and bear rich fruitage. Always there was the reminder that the price is: "Abide in Me; let Me abide in you. Abide in the Word, and let the Word abide in you. Dwell in God; live and move and have your being in God. Seek Him while He may be found."

Gradually, it dawned on me that all Scripture was revealing to the world that "man, whose breath is in his nostrils," man separate and apart from God, is not to be accounted of, for he is nothing. I began to understand why Christ Jesus could say, "I can of mine own self do nothing"—of mine own self I am nothing; "the Father that dwelleth in me, he doeth the works." I could understand St. Paul when he said, "I can do all things through Christ which strengtheneth me," and then I knew what the missing factor was in my life. I had been and was living an ordinary, everyday life. All that God meant to me was an occasional reading of the Bible and an occasional attendance at church. Now I saw that the principle of life, the secret of all successful living, was making God a part of my very consciousness, something which Paul describes as praying without ceasing.

At first, you may not understand why praying without ceasing or thinking about God has anything to do with your being happy, successful, or healthy. You may not even be able to see what connection God has with the mundane affairs of life. This, of course, you are only going to discover through your own experience, because regardless of any testimony I may offer you of what it has done in my life, or in the lives of thousands to whom I have taught this way of life, you will not be convinced until you yourself have had the actual experience.

The reason you are reading this book is because you are being irresistibly drawn to God. There is a compulsion within you to find the missing factor in your life, that which will restore to you your original state of harmony, joy, and peace. Your having read the introduction thus far is an indication that this is what you are seeking; this is the need which clamors for fulfillment in you; and be assured of this: that from now on, your mind will turn again and again to God, until one day, whether sooner or later, it will be made evident to you that your life will only be complete when it is lived in God and has God living in it. You will never feel entirely separate or apart from God because never again in your life will you be able to go for long periods without bringing God into your conscious awareness and in some measure, abiding in Him.

Think for one moment of what is taking place in the mind of the person who awakens in the morning and realizes, "Without God, I am nothing; but with God, all the powers of harmony unite in me to express themselves"; or who ponders some scriptural passage such as, "He performeth the thing that is appointed for me. ... The Lord will perfect that which concerneth me. ... Whither shall I go from thy spirit? or whither shall I flee from thy presence? If I ascend up into heaven, thou art there: if I make my bed in hell, behold, thou art there. ... Yea, though I walk through the valley of the shadow of death, I will fear no evil: for thou art with me." Think of what it means to a businessman, leaving for his office, or to a mother, sending her children off to school, to know that they are not alone—wherever they are, the Spirit of God is with them, and where that Spirit of God is, there is liberty. Never again can they feel alone or that their life is dependent wholly on what they do or what others may do to them, for good or evil, for never again can they forget that there is a *He,* closer than breathing, nearer than hands or feet; there is a Presence which goes before them to make the crooked places straight, a Presence and a Power which goes to prepare a place for them. Never can they be separated from the Spirit of God as long as the Spirit of God is kept alive within them.

As you contemplate this, you will begin to discover that whether you are one of those who pray in holy mountains or in great temples in Jerusalem, or whether you do not pray in any particular place, the truth is that the place whereon you stand is holy ground as long as you are contemplating the presence and the power of God within you. That does not mean that you may not continue to worship in the church of your choice. This book is not meant to take you out of any church where, at the present time, you may be enjoying the association of those on your particular religious path, nor is it meant to put you into any church in which you may not already be worshiping. Its purpose is to reveal the kingdom of God—where it is and how to achieve it. The Master said that the kingdom of God is neither "lo here! nor lo there!" but is within you, and you will learn, through this study, that that kingdom is established in you the very moment that you begin to contemplate His presence and His power within you.

God *is;* of that you may be sure. This is only true in your experience, however, in the degree in which you contemplate, meditate, and keep your mind stayed on God, living, moving, and having your being in the conscious realization that God will never leave you nor forsake you. God's grace is your sufficiency, but this is only made practical in your life by your contemplation of that grace. Only in the degree that you live consciously in the realization of God and let this realization of God dwell in you, does it become true that you do not live alone—that the place whereon you stand is holy ground, for God is with you and He will never leave you nor forsake you.

Every person who has known dissatisfaction, incompleteness, and frustration will some day learn that there is only one missing link in his entire chain of harmonious living. That is the practice of the presence of God—consciously, daily and hourly, abiding in some great spiritual truth of scripture, and it makes no difference which scripture: Christian, Hebrew, Hindu, Buddhist, Taoist, or Muslim. The word of God, given to man through inspired saints, sages, seers, or revelators—this is what we need, in any language, from any country, just as long as it is a universal truth.

I have been a traveler for nearly fifty years, and I have found peace, joy, and companionship wherever I have journeyed. In my opinion, the reason I have enjoyed such satisfying experiences around the globe is because I have carried with me the great truth given us by the Master, "Call no man your father upon the earth: for one is your Father, which is in heaven." This truth has been my passport and has been the open sesame to freedom and joy in all countries, for wherever I have traveled, I have consciously remembered that God is the Father, the creative Principle, the life of all with whom

I come in contact. No one can change the fact that whatever the name, nationality, race, or creed, there is only one God, one Father, and that we are all children of that one Father; but this truth serves only those who consciously remember it, realize it, believe it, and trust it.

In my lifetime, I have known abundance and the absence of abundance, but in every case, whenever there has been a lack of any kind, harmony, wholeness, and completeness have been restored through the realization that "man shall not live by bread alone, but by every word that proceedeth out of the mouth of God. ... I have meat to eat that ye know not of." Have you ever wondered what the Master meant by those words? Over the years, I have spent weeks and months pondering them, sometimes weeks at a time, and the next year more weeks, until I understood their meaning. I realized that he was talking about an inner substance, which made meat on the outer plane of comparative unimportance—not that he would not eat in due time, but when there were more important things to do, he had another kind of meat and bread to sustain him.

After the years that I have spent in this work, I can say to you that the inner meat, the inner water, the inner wine, and the bread of life—all these are brought into tangible experience through inner communion and in no other way. They cannot be brought from the outside into the inside. Not even reading the Bible will do this for you. It is taking the truths of the Bible into meditation and gaining an inner realization of them which changes the words that you read in a book into the word of life, the bread of life, the meat, the wine, and the water of life.

Spiritual truth in a Bible is only a power in proportion as it is brought alive in your consciousness and kept alive.

This is not my word to you; this is the word of the masters who have told us that we shall be kept in peace by keeping our mind stayed on God and that if we abide in the word of God and let the word abide in us we shall bear fruit richly. We shall then have an inner water, an inner wine, an inner meat, and an inner bread to bring to the development and the growth of the fruit that is to appear in the without. You can only feed the tree of life from within, not from without.

The bread of life, the meat, the wine, the water—these are formed inside of us through the contemplation of God, the things of God, and the word of God. These are formed within us by communion with the Spirit. Always remember: The Spirit of God is within you, but it is only the few today who seem capable of spending hours with spiritual literature, and more hours in inner communion—only the few. Their earnest desire to know God will insure their success on the spiritual path.

The message of this book is not a personal message. It is an age-old wisdom that man shall not live by bread alone but by every word remembered in consciousness, by every word and thought of God held within us. By this we live. When we try to live without God, we are living only with the carnal weapons of this world. When, however, we take this great truth into our consciousness and let it abide in us, then we are clad in spiritual armor, and the only sword we need is the sword of the Spirit. And what is the sword of the Spirit except every word that proceedeth out of the mouth of God?

I have learned, and so I endeavor to pass on to you: Keep the word of God alive in your mind, in your thought, and in your experience, and you will never know lack or limitation. Keep consciously before you the truth that no man on earth is your father—there is only one Father, the creative Principle of all mankind—and you will never know anything but love from the men and women of this world.

As you keep the word of God alive in your consciousness, you are practicing the principles of spiritual living. In this book, you will find an exposition of these principles, which I refer to from time to time as the "letter of truth." In and of itself, this is not sufficient "for the letter killeth, but the spirit giveth life."

This book is my personal life revealed. This book, *The Art of Meditation*, and *Living The Infinite Way* reveal all that has happened to me in my entire spiritual career, and not only to me but to all those who have been taught in this way, whether by me or by any other spiritual teacher on this particular path. For it is not I alone who have learned this secret of the Master; it is an ancient wisdom lived many times by many men. Throughout all centuries, this way of life has been practiced, but it has been lost except to those few who live the mystical life.

The world's troubles in these past generations have driven men to seek that which will restore the lost years of the locusts, that which will establish peace on earth and good will to men. I have found it—and in this book, you will find it.

VII

LOVE THY NEIGHBOR

Thou shalt love the Lord thy God with all thy heart, and with all thy soul, and with all thy mind.

This is the first and great commandment.

And the second is like unto it, Thou shalt love thy neighbour as thyself.

Matthew 22:37–39

T HE TWO GREAT commandments of the Master form the basis of our work. In the first and great commandment, we are taught that there is no power apart from God. Our realization must always be that the Father within us, the Infinite Invisible, is our life, our soul, our supply, our fortress, and our high tower. Next in importance is the commandment to "love thy neighbor as thyself," and its corollary that we should "do unto others as we would have others do unto us."

What is love in the spiritual sense? What is the love which is God? As we remember how God was with Abraham, with Moses in the wilderness, with Jesus, John, and Paul, ministering to them, the word "love" takes on a new meaning. We see that this love is not something far-off, nor is it anything that can come to us. It is already a part of our being, already established within us; and more than that, it is universal and impersonal. As this universal and impersonal love flows out from us, we begin to love our neighbor, because it

79

is impossible to feel this love for God within us and not love our fellow man.

> If a man say, I love God, and hateth his brother, he is a liar: for he that loveth not his brother whom he hath seen, how can he love God whom he hath not seen?
>
> I John 4:20

God and man are one, and there is no way to love God without some of that love flowing out to our neighbor.

Let us understand that anything of which we can become aware is a neighbor, whether it appears as a person, place, or thing. Every idea in consciousness is a neighbor. We can love that neighbor as we see him or it possessing no power except that which comes from God. When we see God as the cause and our neighbor as that which is in and of God, then we are loving our neighbor, whether that neighbor appears as a friend, relative, enemy, animal, flower, or stone. In such loving, which understands all neighbors to be of God, derived of God-substance, we find that every idea in consciousness takes its rightful place. Those neighbors who are a part of our experience find their way to us, and those who are not are removed. Let us resolve loving our neighbor into a spiritual activity, beholding love as the substance of all that is, no matter what the form may be. As we rise above our humanhood to a higher dimension of life in which we understand our neighbor to be pure spiritual being, God-governed, neither good nor bad, we are truly loving.

Love is the law of God. When we are in tune with divine Love, loving whether it be friend or enemy, then love is a gentle thing bringing peace. But it is gentle only while we are in tune with it. It is like electricity. Electricity is very gentle and kind, giving light, warmth, and energy, as long as the laws of electricity are obeyed. The minute they are violated or played with, electricity becomes a double-edged sword. The law of love is as inexorable as the law of electricity.

Now let us be very clear on one point: We cannot harm anybody, and nobody can harm us. No one can injure us, but we injure ourselves by a violation of the law of love. The penalty is always upon the one who is doing the evil, never upon the one to whom it is done. The injustice we do to another reacts upon ourselves; the theft from another robs ourselves. The law of love makes it inevitable that the person who seems to have been harmed is really blessed. He has a greater opportunity to rise than ever before, and usually some greater benefit comes to him than he had ever dreamed possible; whereas the perpetrator of the evil deed is haunted by memories until that day comes when he can forgive himself. The whole proof that this is true is in the one word "Self." God is our Selfhood. God is my Selfhood and God is your Selfhood. God constitutes my being, for God is my life, my soul, my spirit, my mind, and my activity. God is my Self. That Self is the only Self there is—my Self and your Self. If I rob your Self, whom am I robbing? My Self. If I lie about your Self, about whom am I lying? My Self. If I cheat your Self, whom do I cheat? My Self. There is only one Self, and that which I do to another, I do to my Self.

The Master taught this lesson in the twenty-fifth chapter of Matthew, when he said: "Inasmuch as ye have done it unto one of the least of these my brethren, ye have done it unto me." What I do of good for you, I am not doing for you at all; it is for my benefit. What I do of evil to you, will not hurt you, for you will find a way to recover from it; the reaction will be on me. We must come to the place where we actually believe and can say with our whole heart: "There is only one Self. The injustice that I am doing to another I am doing to myself. The lack of thoughtfulness that I show to another, I am showing to myself." In such recognition, the true meaning of doing unto others as we would have them do unto us is revealed.

God is individual being, which means that God is the only Self, and there is no way for any hurt or evil to enter to defile the infinite purity of the Soul of God, nor anything at which evil can strike or to which it can attach itself. When the Master repeated the age-old wisdom: "Therefore all things whatsoever ye would that men should do to you, do ye even so to them: for this is the law and the prophets," he was giving us a principle. Unless we do unto others as we would have others do unto us, we injure, not the others, but ourselves. In this present state of human consciousness, it is true that the evil thoughts, dishonest acts, and thoughtless words we inflict upon others do harm them temporarily, but always, in the end, it will be found that the injury was not nearly so great to them as it was to ourselves.

In the days to come, when men recognize the great truth that God is the Selfhood of every individual, the evil aimed at us from another will never touch us, but will immediately rebound upon the one who sends it. In the degree that we recognize God as our individual being, we realize that no weapon that is formed against us can prosper because the only *I* is God. There will be no fear of what man can do to us, since our Selfhood is God and cannot be harmed. As soon as the first realization of this truth comes to us, we no longer concern ourselves with what our neighbor does to us. Morning, noon, and night we must watch our thoughts, our words, and our deeds to make certain that we, ourselves, are not responsible for anything of a negative nature which would have undesirable repercussions.

This will not result in our being good because we fear evil consequences. The revelation of the one Self goes far deeper than that: It enables us to see that God is our Selfhood, and that anything of an erroneous or negative nature which emanates from any individual has power only in the degree that we ourselves give it power. So it is that whatever of good or of evil we do unto others, we do unto the Christ of our own being. "Inasmuch as ye have done it unto one of the least of these my brethren, ye have done it unto me." In that realization, we shall see that this is the truth about all men, and that the only road to a successful and satisfying life is to understand our neighbor to be our Self.

The Master has instructed us specifically as to the ways in which we can serve our fellow man. He emphasized the idea of service. His whole mission was the healing of the sick, the raising of the dead, and the feeding of the poor. The moment that we make ourselves avenues for the outflow of divine Love, from that very moment, we begin serving each other, expressing love, devotion, and sharing, all in the name of the Father.

Let us follow the example of the Master and seek no glory for ourselves. With him, always, it was the Father who doeth the works. There is never any room for self-justification, or self-righteousness, or self-glorification in the performance of any kind of service. Sharing with one another should not be reduced to mere philanthropy. Some people wonder why they find themselves left with nothing when they have always been so charitable. They come upon lean days because they believe that they have given of their own possessions, whereas the truth is that "the earth is the Lord's and the fullness thereof." If we express our love for our fellow man, realizing that we are giving nothing of ourselves, but all is of the Father, from whom every good and perfect gift comes, we shall then be able to give freely and discover that with all our giving there yet remain twelve basketfuls left over. To believe that we are giving of our property, our time, or our strength reduces such giving to philanthropy and brings with it no reward. The true giving comes when giving is a recognition that "the earth is the Lord's," and that whether we give of our time or our effort, we are not giving of our own, but of the Lord's. Then are we expressing the love which is of God.

As we forgive, divine Love is flowing out from us. As we pray for our enemies, we are loving divinely. Praying for our friends profiteth nothing. The greatest rewards of prayer come when we learn to set aside specific periods every day to pray for those who despitefully use us, to pray for those who persecute us, to pray for those who are our enemies—not only personal enemies because there are some people who have no personal enemies, but religious, racial, or national enemies. We learn to pray, "Father, forgive them; for they know not what they do." When we pray for our enemies, when we pray that their eyes be opened to the truth, many times these enemies become our friends.

We begin this practice with our personal relationships. If there are individuals with whom we are not on harmonious terms, we find, as we turn within and pray that brotherly love and harmony be established between us, that instead of enemies, we come into a relationship of spiritual brotherhood with them. Our relationship with everybody then takes on a harmony and a heretofore unknown joy.

This is not possible as long as we feel antagonism toward anyone. If we are harboring within us personal animosity, or if we are indulging in national or religious hatred, prejudice, or bigotry, our prayers are worthless. We must go to God with clean hands in order to pray, and to approach God with clean hands, we must relinquish our animosities. Within ourselves, we must, first of all, pray the prayer of forgiveness for those who have offended us, since they know not what they do; and secondly, acknowledge within ourselves: "I stand in relationship to God as a son, and therefore, I stand in relationship to every man as a brother." When we have established that state of purity within ourselves, then we can ask the Father:

Give me grace; give me understanding; give me peace; give me this day my daily bread—give me this day spiritual bread, spiritual understanding. Give me forgiveness, even for those harmless trespasses which I have unwittingly committed.

The person who turns within for light, for grace, for understanding, and for forgiveness never fails in his prayers.

The law of God is the law of love, the law of loving our enemies—not fearing them, not hating them, but loving them. No matter what an individual does to us, we are not to strike back. To resist evil, to retaliate, or to seek revenge is to acknowledge evil as reality. If we resist evil, if we refute it, if we avenge ourselves, or if we strike back, we are not praying for them which despitefully use us and persecute us.

How can we say that we acknowledge good alone, God, as the only power, if we hate our neighbor or do evil to anyone? Christ is the true identity and to recognize an identity other than Christ is to withdraw ourselves from Christ-consciousness.

> Love your enemies, bless them that curse you, do good to them that hate you, and pray for them which despitefully use you, and persecute you;
>
> That ye may be the children of your Father which is in heaven: for he maketh his sun to rise on the evil and on the good, and sendeth rain on the just and on the unjust.
>
> Matthew 5:44, 45

There is no other way to be the Christ, the Son of God. The Christ-mind has in it no criticism, no judgment, no condemnation, but beholds the Christ of God as the activity of individual being, as your soul and mine. Human eyes do not comprehend this because as human beings, we are good and bad; but spiritually, we are the Sons of God, and through spiritual consciousness, we can discern the spiritual good in each other. There is no room in spiritual living for persecution, hatred, judgment, or condemnation of any person or group of people. It is not only inconsistent, but hypocritical to talk about the Christ and our great love for God in one breath, and, in the next breath, speak disparagingly of a neighbor who is of a different race, creed, nationality, political affiliation, or economic status. One cannot be the child of God as long as he persecutes or hates anyone or anything, but only as he lives in a consciousness of no judgment or condemnation.

The usual interpretation of "judge not" is that we are not to judge evil of anyone. We must go much further than that; we dare not judge good of anyone either. We must be as careful not to call anyone good as we are not to call anyone evil. We should not label anyone or anything as evil, but likewise, we should not label anyone or anything as good. The Master said: "Why callest thou me good? there is none good but one, that is God." It is the height of egotism to say: "I am good; I have understanding; I am moral; I am generous; I am benevolent." If any qualities of good are manifesting through us, let us not call ourselves good, but recognize these qualities as the activity of God. "Son, thou art ever with me, and all that I have is thine." All the good of the Father is expressed through me.

One of the basic principles of The Infinite Way is that good humanhood is not sufficient to ensure our entry into the spiritual kingdom nor to bring us into oneness with cosmic law. It is undoubtedly better to be a good human being than a bad one, just as it is better to be a healthy human being than a sick one, but achieving health or achieving goodness, in and of itself, is not spiritual living. Spiritual living comes only when we have risen above human good and human evil and realize: "There are not good human beings or bad human beings. Christ is the only identity." Then we look out on the world and see neither good men and women nor bad men and women, but recognize Christ alone as the reality of being.

> Therefore if thou bring thy gift to the altar, and there rememberest that thy brother hath ought against thee;
>
> Leave there thy gift before the altar, and go thy way; first be reconciled to thy brother, and then come and offer thy gift.
>
> Matthew 5:23, 24

If we are holding anyone in condemnation as a human being, good or bad, just or unjust, we have not made peace with our brother and we are not ready for the prayer of communion with the Infinite. We rise above the righteousness of the scribes and Pharisees only when we stop seeing good and evil, and stop boasting about goodness as if any of us could be good. Goodness is a quality and activity of God alone, and because it is, it is universal.

Let us never accept a human being into our consciousness who needs healing, employing, or enriching because if we do, we are his enemy instead of his friend. If there is any man, woman, or child we believe to be sick, sinning, or dying, let us do no praying until we have made peace with that brother. The peace we must make with that brother is to ask forgiveness for making the mistake of sitting in judgment on any individual because everyone is God in expression. All is God manifested. God alone constitutes this universe; God constitutes the life, the mind, and the soul of every individual.

"Thou shalt not bear false witness against thy neighbor" has a much broader connotation than merely not spreading rumors or indulging in gossip about our neighbor. We are not to hold our neighbor in humanhood. If we say, "I have a good neighbor," we are bearing false witness against him just as much as if we said, "I have a bad neighbor," because we are acknowledging a state of humanhood, sometimes good and sometimes bad, but never spiritual. To bear false witness against our neighbor is to declare that he is human, that he is finite, that he has failings, that he is something less than the very Son of God. Every time we acknowledge humanhood, we violate cosmic law. Every time we acknowledge our neighbor as sinful, poor, sick, or dead, every time we acknowledge him to be other than the Son of God, we are bearing false witness against our neighbor.

In the violation of that cosmic law, we bring about our own punishment. God does not punish us. We punish ourselves because if I say that you are poor, I virtually am saying that I am poor. There is only one *I* and one Selfhood; whatever truth I know about you is the truth about me. If I accept the belief of poverty in the world, that reacts upon me. If I say that you are sick or that you are not kind, I am accepting a quality apart from God, an activity apart from God, and in that way I am condemning myself because there is but one Self. Ultimately, I convict myself by bearing false witness against my neighbor and I am the one who suffers the consequences.

The only way to avoid bearing false witness against our neighbor is to realize that the Christ is our neighbor, that our neighbor is a spiritual being, the Son of God, just as we are. He may not know it; we may not know it, but the truth is: I am Spirit; I am Soul; I am Consciousness; I am God expressed—and so is he, whether he is good or bad, friend or enemy, next door or across the seas.

In the Sermon on the Mount, the Master gave us a guide and a code of human conduct to follow while developing spiritual consciousness. The Infinite Way emphasizes spiritual values, a spiritual code, which automatically results in good humanhood. Good humanhood is a natural consequence of spiritual identification. It would be difficult to understand that the Christ is the soul and the life of individual being, and then quarrel with our neighbor or slander him. We place our faith, trust, and confidence in the Infinite Invisible, and we do not take into consideration human circumstances and conditions. Then, when we do come to human circumstances or conditions, we see them in their true relationship. When we say, "Thou shalt love thy neighbor as thyself," we are not speaking of human love, affection, or friendliness; we are holding our neighbor in spiritual identity, and then we see the effect of this right identification in the human picture.

Many times we find it difficult to love our neighbor because we believe that our neighbor is standing between us and our good. Let me assure you that this is far from true. No outer influence for good or evil can act upon us. We ourselves release our good. To understand the full meaning of this requires a transition in consciousness. As human beings, we think that there are those individuals in the world who can, if they would, be good to us; or we think that there are some who are an influence for evil, harm, or destruction.

How can this possibly be true if God is the only influence in our life—God, who is "closer ... than breathing, and nearer than hands or feet"? The only influence is that of the Father within, which is always good. "Thou couldest have no power at all against me, except it were given thee from above."

When we realize that our life is unfolding from within our own being, we come to the realization that no one on earth has ever hurt us, and no one on earth has ever helped us. Every hurt that has ever come into our experience has been the direct result of our inability to behold this universe as spiritual. We have looked upon it with either praise or condemnation, and no matter which it was, we have brought a penalty upon ourselves. If we look back over the years, we could almost blueprint the reasons for every bit of discord that has come into our experience. In every case, it is the same thing—always because we saw somebody or something that was not spiritual.

Nobody can benefit us; nobody can harm us. It is what goes out from us that returns to bless or to condemn us. We create good and we create evil. We create our own good and we create our own evil. God does not do either: God *is*. God is a principle of love. If we are at-one with that principle, then we bring good into our experience; but if we are not at-one with that principle, we bring evil into our experience. Whatever is flowing out from our consciousness, that which is going forth in secret, is being shown to the world in outward manifestation.

Whatever emanates from God in the consciousness of man, individually or collectively, is power. What is it that emanates from God and operates in the consciousness of man but love, truth, completeness, perfection, wholeness— all of the Christ-qualities? Because there is only one God, one infinite power, love must be the controlling emotion in the hearts and souls of every person on the face of the globe.

Now, in contrast to that, are those other thoughts of fear, doubt, hate, jealousy, envy, and animality, which are probably uppermost in the consciousness of many of the people of the world. We, as truth-seekers, belong to a very small minority of those who have received the impartation that the evil thoughts of men are not power; they have no control over us. Not all the evil or false thinking on earth has any power over you or over me when we understand that love is the only power. There is no power in hate; there is no power in animosity; there is no power in resentment, lust, greed, or jealousy.

There are few people in the world who are able to accept the teaching that love is the only power and who are willing to "become as a little child." Those who do accept this basic teaching of the Master, however, are those of whom he said:

> ... I thank thee, O Father, Lord of heaven and earth, that thou hast hid these things from the wise and prudent, and hast revealed them unto babes: even so, Father; for so it seemed good in thy sight.
>
> ... Blessed are the eyes which see the things that ye see:
>
> For I tell you, that many prophets and kings have desired to see those things which ye see, and have not seen them; and to hear those things which ye hear, and have not heard them.

> Luke 10:21, 23, 24

Once we accept this all-important teaching of the Master and our eyes see beyond the appearance, we shall consciously realize daily that every person in the world is empowered with love from on High and that the love in his consciousness is the only power, a power of good unto you, unto me, and unto himself; but that the evil in human thought, whether it takes the form of greed, jealousy, lust, or mad ambition, is not power, is not to be feared or hated.

Our method of loving our brother as ourselves is in this realization: The good in our brother is of God and is power; the evil in our brother is not power, not power against us, and in the last analysis, not even power against him, once he awakens to the truth. To love our brother means to know the truth about our brother: to know that that in him, which is of God, is power and that in him, which is not of God, is not power. Then are we truly loving our brother. Centuries of orthodox teaching have instilled in all the peoples of the world a sense of separation so that they have developed interests separate and apart from one another and also apart from the world at large. When we master the principle of oneness, however, and this principle becomes a conviction deep within us, in that oneness, the lion and the lamb can lie down together.

This is proved to be true through an understanding of the correct meaning of the word "I." Once we catch the first perception of the truth that the *I* of me is the *I* of you, the Self of me is the Self of you, then we shall see why we have no interests apart from each other. There would be no wars, no conflicts of any kind, if only it could be made clear that the real being of everybody in the universe is the one God, the one Christ, the one Soul, and the one Spirit. What benefits one benefits another because of this oneness.

In that spiritual oneness, we find our peace with one another. If we experiment with this we shall quickly see how true it is. When we go to the market, we realize that everyone we meet is this same one that we are, that the same life animates him, the same soul, the same love, the same joy, the same peace, the same desire for good. In other words, the same God sits enthroned within all those with whom we come in contact. They may not, at the moment, be conscious of this divine Presence within their being, but they will respond as we recognize It in them. In the business world, whether it is among our co-workers, our employers, or our employees, whether it is among competitors, or whether in management and labor relationships, we maintain this attitude of recognition:

I am you. My interest is your interest; your interest is mine, since the one Life animates our being, the one Soul, the one Spirit of God. Anything we do for each other, we do because of the principle that binds us together.

A difference is immediately noticeable in our business relationships, in our relationships with tradespeople, and in our community relationships—ultimately, in national and international relationships. The moment that we give up our human sense of separateness, this principle becomes operative in our experience. It has never failed and it never will fail to bring forth rich fruitage.

Everyone is here on earth but for one purpose, and that purpose is to show forth the glory of God, the divinity and the fullness of God. In that realization, we shall be brought into contact only with those who are a blessing to us as we are a blessing to them.

The moment we look to a person for our good, we may find good today and evil tomorrow. Spiritual good may come *through* you to me from the Father, but it does not come *from* you. You cannot be the source of any good to me, but the Father may use you as an instrument for Its good to flow through you to me. So, as we look at our friends or our family in this light, they become instruments of God, of God's good, reaching us through them. We come under grace by taking the position that all good emanates from the Father within. It may appear to come through countless different people, but it is an emanation of good, of God from within us.

What is the principle? "Love thy neighbor as thyself." In obeying this commandment, we love friend and foe; we pray for our enemies; we forgive, though it be seventy times seven; we bear not false witness against our neighbor by holding him in condemnation; we judge not as to good or evil, but see through every appearance to the Christ-identity—the one Self which is your Self and my Self. Then can it be said of us:

> ... Come, ye blessed of my Father, inherit the kingdom prepared for you from the foundation of the world:
>
> For I was an hungred, and ye gave me meat: I was thirsty, and ye gave me drink: I was a stranger, and ye took me in:
>
> Naked, and ye clothed me: I was sick, and ye visited me: I was in prison, and ye came unto me.
>
> Then shall the righteous answer him, saying, Lord, when saw we thee an hungred, and fed thee? or thirsty, and gave thee drink?
>
> When saw we thee a stranger, and took thee in? or naked, and clothed thee?
>
> Or when saw we thee sick, or in prison, and came unto thee?
>
> And the King shall answer and say unto them, Verily I say unto you, Inasmuch as ye have done it unto one of the least of these my brethren, ye have done it unto me.

Matthew 25:34–40

VIII

GOD IS ONE

Hear, O Israel: The Lord our God is one Lord.

Deuteronomy 6: 4

IN OUR AGREEMENT and understanding that God is One, God has no opposite, and there is no opposition. With God as One, there is only one activity, one being, one cause, one power, one law.

When the Master was asked which of the commandments was the greatest, he answered, "Thou shalt love the Lord thy God with all thy heart, and with all thy soul, and with all thy mind." Therefore, the first and greatest commandment is, "Thou shalt have none other gods before me." We think of God as power, and so the commandment is: Thou shalt acknowledge no other power but God. What, then, are we fearing—germs, infection, contagion? Since God is the only power, can these things have any power? According to the Master's teaching, they could have no power except such as was given them by God.

Do we fear lack or limitation? How can lack or limitation affect us? Do we fear wars and hydrogen bombs? According to the first commandment, only God is power. What would happen to the power of the hydrogen bomb if we could realize God as the only power? Think on this deeply, because there must come a moment of transition when we can intellectually declare, "Why, that is right. If God is the only

95

power, what have we to fear from all the so-called powers of earth and hell?" Then there must come a moment of transition when we go from that intellectual agreement to spiritual agreement, a feeling of agreement within, "Yes, that is the truth; I feel the truth of that one power."

"Thou shalt have none other gods before me"—therefore, God is the only law. We are now faced with a startling question: Is there a law of disease? God is the only law. What, then, is causing disease? What is perpetuating it, if there is no law of disease? We are told in Scripture, "According to your faith be it unto you"; and therefore, if you have confidence, faith, or belief that there is a law of disease, so it must be unto you. You see, the world is trying to remove disease through the study of the laws of disease, and there are no such laws.

According to the Master's teaching and the teaching of all spiritual wisdom throughout the ages, there is only one power, one law, one being. Think, now, because this is the point to which we are leading: There is nothing in all this world to use God-power for or against. Since there is no power apart from God, there is no sin, no evil; since there is no law apart from God, there is no law of disease, no law of lack or limitation, and we no longer have to turn to God to overcome these things, to help us rise above them, to destroy, correct, or remove them.

That is the function of this teaching, the teaching which we may call a teaching of *is*—just the two letters *i-s, is*—and it is just as simple as the revelation which brought The Infinite Way into existence, also a two-letter word a-s, *as*. God is expressed, manifest, as you and as me; God is appearing as your being and my being; God is appearing as, God manifest as, this universe. There is no selfhood apart from God since

God appears as this universe; there is no condition apart from God since God appears as the substance and activity of this universe. God appearing *as*, logically leads up to God *is*. *Is* has no point of comparison since it always, eternally and immortally, is what it *is*, and that *is*, is Spirit. It is not some degree of human good, nor is it some degree of human evil. It *is*—spiritually, harmoniously, joyously, eternally, immortally, infinitely *is*. *Is*.

Law *is*. There is not good law or bad law. There is only law—God *is*. There is not good or strong power, not good or evil power. There is only power—God *is*. There is no power to oppose anything, so there is no use praying to it to overcome our enemies, no use praying to it to overcome sin or sinful desires or appetites, no use praying to it to overcome disease, since there is only one power and the power that is, is God.

We must be arriving now, at a state of consciousness called *Is*, and we must rest in that *Is*. We have no evil to oppose or from which to be protected, and we do not have to pray in order to get God to do something for us, since God, Good, already *is*. If, deep within us, we can feel a responsive agreement, that is our prayer, our treatment, and our communion with God. "Hear, O Israel: The Lord our God is one Lord"—one in essence, one in cause, one in effect, one infinite Good.

You are led into a continuing state of consciousness in which you do not, even by suggestion, think of turning to God to do something for you, since that of which you are thinking already *is*. Never do you pray for something or someone. Your whole prayer becomes an inner agreement that it already *is* and always has been. "Before Abraham was, I am.... lo, I am with you always, even unto the end of the world.... I will never leave thee, nor forsake thee." *Is, am, is*—I am with you; it *is* so. No longer do you reach mentally for some statement of truth. There is now only one statement of truth, and it comes in one word, *is*. It already *is*.

Many, many years ago it was revealed to me, "That which I am seeking, I am. I already am; it already *is;* it always *is*." With that understanding came the realization that I could give up seeking, I could give up searching, I could even give up praying. It already *is*. And now my prayer is no longer asking or affirming. My prayer is the realization, the recognition, of *is*.

Whatever good has come into your consciousness in the form of desire or hope already *is*. There is no power to bring it to you tomorrow. The question of time enters here. You cannot live yesterday, can you? No good can come into your experience yesterday, and so far as we know, no one has ever lived tomorrow. The spiritual literature of the world seems very much in accord that now is the only time we live, that now is the only time we will live, and for that reason, now is the only time.

So you can see, prayer that would have to do with yesterday or last year, or perhaps the last incarnation, would be a waste of time. You will never live an hour ago, so there is no use praying for or about anything that concerns itself with an hour ago. "Let the dead bury their dead." Let yesterday bury yesterday, and let us concern ourselves with now. Since we cannot live tomorrow there is no reason to wish or to desire or to hope for tomorrow. There is only one time in which our prayers can materialize, and that time is now.

It is for this reason that we must learn and understand the instantaneousness and the spontaneity of healing and reformation, since it can only take place now. What great fact do we discover? Above all, we discover that *I am*. *I am now*. You will ask, "What is *I am?*" That, you must learn from within, but one thing is certain: If *I am*, all that the Father is, and all that the Father has, *is* right now in that *I am-ness*. All that the Father has is now. All that the Father has is mine now. All that the Father is, *I am*, now. If you are able to follow this, you are feeling, "Why, that is just *is* again; *is*—not to be hoped for and not to be prayed for. Why not? Because in this now there is only one power, the one presence, the one law, which *I am*. All that God is, *I am* now."

So far as we know, the Master never prayed for anything for himself. Can you understand why he never seemed to have a need? If it came to healing, he could heal multitudes; if it came to supply, he could take care of multitudes. At no point was he seeking to get or to acquire. The Bible states that he was "an hungred," that he was tempted to turn the stones into bread. Was he tempted to believe in lack? No. He recognized his fulfillment, he recognized his divine Sonship, he recognized that all that the Father had was his now and that he did not have to make it so. It already *is*. "Get thee behind me, Satan." Get behind me—the temptation to believe that I can acquire something a minute from now, when in this *nowness* is my *isness*. It is now. *I am*. All that God is, *I am*.

Surely, deep within your consciousness comes the feeling of agreement that right now *I am* in the midst of you; all that ever has been is now; all that ever will be is now, for now is the only time—the divine harmony of God is your being now, and that is your prayer.

So, once again, we are admonished to withhold all judgment because if we judge by appearances, the world is full of skies that sit on mountains or car tracks that come together.

Yet these are only appearances or illusions, only temptations to keep us from venturing forth.

You can readily see that you cannot discuss this with friends or relatives because they live by appearances, and appearances are the very bread and butter of their daily living. All of the conversation of humanhood is about appearances, so it is useless trying to talk, argue, or reason this out with them. Be still and know, but be very still. Be very still and spiritually know that this is the truth: There is no law of disease; there is no evil; there is no power that can harm. Spiritually feel the rightness of this. If you feel it spiritually, you are praying aright rather than praying amiss. If you can feel the rightness of the one law, the one presence, the one power—that there is nothing to overcome, nothing to destroy or to remove—then you will know, "*I* already am. It *is*; God *is*; harmony *is*."

As we walk through the experiences of each day, temptations to judge as to good or bad, sick or well, rich or poor, sin or purity will continually arise. We are faced, not only with the Master's three temptations but with three million. There is always the temptation to look at the woman taken in adultery and throw a few stones or at the thief caught in the act and judge. From morning to night, we are tempted to believe in appearances and to label them good or bad, right or wrong, but we must resist these temptations by learning to look at person, circumstance, condition, or disease, and withhold judgment. We must realize *is*—*is*—and let the Father define, outline, and show forth that which spiritually *is*. "My kingdom is not of this world." There is no use trying to judge the spiritual kingdom from appearances—it will not work.

The study and practice of The Infinite Way is the development of spiritual consciousness. It is not going through human existence picking out all the wrong things and finding a system whereby to make them right. It is looking through the appearance of both human good and human evil, and learning to behold the spiritual reality which *is*, even where the appearance seems to be.

About 500 B.C., Lao-Tzu stated, "A name cannot name the eternal. Nameless, it is the source of Heaven and Earth; with names one comes to creation and things." In other words, if you can name God, it is not God. And so it is that anything that you could think about God would represent only your concept of God. If you say, "God is love," that is a concept of God; it is not God. So praying to Love or to Mind would be praying to concepts, not to God. You could go through all the synonyms for God and declare that God is this or that, and you would be wrong. That would not be God at all; it would be only a concept of God, and praying to it would bring no results. Since any thought that you might think about God would represent an opinion, a theory, or a concept and would not be God, how then are we in The Infinite Way to consider God? Actually, there is only one thing that you can know about God—God *is*. Of that you can be very sure.

You have no way of knowing whether God is mind, or God is life, or God is love. These may be quotations that merely represent ideas formulated by the saints, seers, and sages down through the ages. They may be perfectly correct in their estimate of what God is, but you will have to admit that anything that may be said about God represents a theory, a belief, an opinion, or a concept—all except one thing: God *is*. That you know—God *is*. "In all thy ways acknowledge

Him, and He shall direct thy paths.... Thou wilt keep him in perfect peace, whose mind is stayed on thee." Acknowledge Him and keep your mind stayed on the God that *is*. God *is*. That is enough to know. What more can you do in the way of communion with God than this inner acknowledgment that God *is*? All else may be speculation or opinion, but one thing that no man can take from you is the realization that God *is*. As long as you acknowledge that God *is* and rest in that inner assurance, in some way, mysterious to human sense, God will reveal all that you need to know about God.

We have been leading up to this very important point: Do not be concerned with what anyone teaches about the nature of God, and do not be concerned with what anyone has written about God. Much that you read and study may appear to be right to you; much you may question. There is only one fact about which you can feel complete agreement, about which no doubt will ever enter your thought: God *is*. Be satisfied with that until God reveals to you, from within your own being, what God is, when God is, how God is. Let God reveal Itself to you.

I have had my own inner experience with God, with the realization of God, and with the actual feeling of the presence of God, but I cannot make this real to you. Many could not even believe that I have had the experience. Unless you have had some measure of God-experience, how could you possibly know if I am telling the truth, or whether I, myself, might not be mistaken? I know, but I cannot convey that knowledge to you. On one point you are already in agreement—God *is*. If you willingly accept that *isness* of God, that inner point of awareness and realization that God *is*, and ponder it, soon God will define Itself. God will reveal Itself, unfold and disclose Itself within you in an original way, and with each experience will come some measure of what we call healing.

You will not find health and wealth added to you; you will find that health and wealth have been included in you since "before even Abraham was." You will find that since God is the infinite nature of your being, all harmony and all good are included in the infinitude of that one spiritual being.

This you will experience for yourself, not by believing me and not by accepting my word. I only wish that, by believing me, spiritual wisdom and demonstration could come to you, but it cannot be so. Spiritual experience can come only through your own realization. I can tell you only this: If you, without prejudice or opinion, without a theory or concept of what God is, can realize, "God *is*, that I know," and dwell with that and ponder it, keeping your thought in that line, from out of the depths of your consciousness within will come the experience revealing what God is, and how God operates and acts throughout this marvelous universe. This will be through spiritual discernment, and this will not come merely by agreeing with what others have said or written about God. Spiritual discernment will come with every God-experience, and you can have a God-experience only through knowing the truth. And what is the only truth that you know? God *is*—that is all the spiritual wisdom you know or will know until God reveals more from within your own being.

The ancient Hebrews said, "The Lord our God is one Lord," but that is also a restatement of a concept of God. We go on from there and say that God is one power, one law, but until God, Itself, reveals that, it remains a concept. To me, it is no longer a concept—it is a revealed truth because of an experience that took place in my consciousness, but to you it may be just a statement that I am repeating. One thing you do know—God *is*. Hold that to yourself, live with it, be satisfied with it until, to what you already know, to what you already have of spiritual wisdom, will be added the balance: "For whosoever hath, to him shall be given, and he shall have more abundance." You have this spiritual wisdom that God *is*, and by pondering it, meditating upon it, and thinking upon it within your own being, there will be added unto you all the rest: who God is; what God is; how God is. The way will be made clear to you from within your own being.

I have but one wish for the students of The Infinite Way, and all others on the path, and that is, not that they accept what my experience in and with God has been, but that each one may himself experience God, know God, feel God, love and understand God, and finally realize Godhood.

IX

REALIZATION OF ONENESS
CHAPTER 4

NO *AND!*

THE SECRET OF meeting error lies in knowing its nature. And the nature of error can be summed up in such words as "carnal mind," "suggestion," "appearance," or "hypnotism." The nature of error as hypnotism, or the carnal mind, can be illustrated in this way: If there were a plant in the room where you are now sitting and if someone hypnotized you, he could make you believe that, instead of branches, snakes were growing out of the flowerpot, and you would accept and believe it. Through hypnotic suggestion, the hypnotist has taken temporary control of your mind, and because you are apparently unable to act independently, you follow his suggestion to its logical conclusion. A fear of the snakes is set up in you; you run away from them and may even pick up a knife with which to chop off their heads—all this based on the belief that snakes are actually there.

No matter what you might do to those nonexistent snakes, you still could not change the fact that as long as you remain hypnotized you will see snakes. There is no possible way for you to be rid of those snakes except to become dehypnotized; there is no way to get rid of your fear of snakes except to become dehypnotized; there is no way to put up your sword except to become dehypnotized. In other words, as long as the hypnosis lasts, all the component parts of the picture are there, are they not?

Now just as it is possible to hypnotize you into believing that there are snakes in the room, so is it possible to hypnotize you into believing that there is a selfhood other than God in any place where you happen to be. As soon as you have been hypnotized into believing in a selfhood apart from God, you then logically accept all the beliefs regarding this selfhood: birth, growth, maturity, and ultimately death. There is only one way to be rid of the human picture, and that is to understand that there is no person and there is no selfhood other than God in the room or in any other place. But the hypnotized person will at once counter with, "How can you say that there is only God in the room?" And the answer is simple: there is only one Life, and that Life is God; there is only one Soul, and that Soul is God; there is only one Spirit; there is only one Law; there is only one creative Principle: God. What then can be present except God? Nothing!

The moment you see God *and*, you are hypnotized. The moment you see a mortal, material world, you are hypnotized; and from then on, there is no possible way to get rid of the appearance. That is the reason that even if you kill the snake over there in the flowerpot, two more will rise up to take its place. That is why, with all the advances made in *materia medica*, everybody still dies because everybody who is born must die. They do and they will. At best they may live a few more years, but that is all. People still die of pneumonia; people still die of tuberculosis; they still die of cancer; they still die of heart failure, and were a cure found for these, something else would immediately replace them.

If you can agree that there is God, which means that you accept an infinite power of good, certainly then you must be able to understand that there cannot be error, disease, or death. In fact, not since time began has there ever been a single death in the kingdom of God.

So whatever you see in the nature of sin, disease, or death is a part of the hypnosis, and, furthermore, whatever you see as good humanhood is also a part of the same hypnosis. Even the healthy human being of thirty or forty will some day be an old human being of seventy or eighty. When you see a young, healthy person, therefore, you are just being fooled by an appearance of good. Until you can become dehypnotized to the degree that you know that there are not good human beings or bad human beings, that there are not diseased human beings or healthy human beings, but that there is only God, the one Life, the one Soul, the one Spirit, the one Substance, the one Law, the one Activity—until that time, you will have to experience death.

Judge Not after Appearances

No one can ever be dehypnotized as long as he is judging by appearances because the human mind with which he is judging is a state of hypnotism. In other words, in looking out from our eyes, we are looking out from a state of hypnosis in which our eyes are always going to see babies being born and old people dying; our ears are always going to be hearing about sin, disease, death, lack, and limitation. Until we are able to shut off those five senses and develop an inner discernment, we are always going to see, hear, taste, touch, and smell error.

If we look through our eyes at the people of this world, all we shall ever see are human beings, sometimes good, sometimes bad. The man and wife who love each other one day drive daggers into each other's hearts the next day. The parent who fondles the child one day reproaches him the next. It is the human picture, sometimes good, sometimes evil. That is what we shall always see, hear, taste, touch, and smell with the five physical senses.

The only way to be dehypnotized is to quiet the physical senses, to be still inside, and then spiritual awareness reveals the truth of being that enables us to see that which is not visible, to hear that which is not audible, to know that which is not knowable with the human senses.

A person with no musical appreciation listening to a symphony hears only a mass of dull monotonous noises, but a person with a developed musical consciousness listening to the same symphony hears harmony, melody, and rhythm. What does a person who has no art appreciation see when he looks at a beautiful painting? Daubs of paint. That is all—nothing more, nothing less—just daubs of paint that do not make sense. On the other hand, a person with an appreciation of art sees whatever it is that the artist had in mind, and appreciates the technique, execution, coloring, and the shading.

A person who knows nothing of sculpture looks at a statue, and what does he see? A piece of bronze or marble made into a statue which to him appears only as a very poor likeness. But the person with an artistic sense looks at it, and he sees the skill expressed by the line, form, and rhythm; he sees in it the flow in the artist's mind and hands. Such people are not seeing with their eyes; they are seeing through their understanding of music and art.

And just as no one will ever be able to understand a symphony or a piece of sculpture until he develops a certain measure of artistic appreciation, so no one will ever be able to understand the spiritual universe until he develops that inner spiritual consciousness, that which is called Christ-consciousness. It was Christ-consciousness which enabled Jesus to say to Pilate, the man who had the greatest temporal power of his day in Jerusalem, "Thou couldest have no power at all against me, except it were given thee from above." How could Jesus make such a daring statement in the face of the great temporal power that Pilate wielded? It was only because he had the inner vision to see through to something beyond what the eyes could see and the ears could hear. He knew something that the human being could not know, and he proved it when he allowed himself to be crucified. They could crucify him, but they could not kill him. The crucifixion and the nails had no power.

The Dehypnotized
Consciousness Sees Reality

Dehypnotism is a state of consciousness that sees that which actually is: it is the ability to see, hear, taste, touch, and smell reality; it is the ability to see sin not as sin, and disease not as disease, but rather to be able to separate these from the person and realize that we are dealing with a false appearance produced by the belief in a selfhood apart from God, a universal belief so powerful that it operates as law in our consciousness until we detect and cast it out, that is, until we know the truth which makes us free.

The only way this can be accomplished is through spiritual consciousness. First of all, we must know this: we cannot cure a disease—there is none; we cannot overcome poverty—there is none; we cannot overcome death—there is none. The only thing we can do is to recognize that we are not dealing with those appearances or suggestions as such; we are dealing with hypnotism.

Even a so-called mental cause for a disease is just as much an illusion as is the physical disease. If there is a mental cause for a physical disease, as is claimed in some teachings, the disease is no illusion, since it has a real cause. We, in The Infinite Way, believe that even a mental cause is as much of an illusion as the physical disease since all there is to the human scene is of the nature of illusion. The mental cause is as illusory in its nature as the physical effect.

The truth is that all there is, is infinite God and Its creation. There is nothing else. To understand reality, we must understand that Spirit alone is real, since Spirit is infinite. All that exists, then, must exist at the standpoint of Spirit and be under spiritual law. Therefore, we are not dealing with the physical effects of mental causes: We are dealing only with God manifesting Itself and expressing Its infinite harmonies, and with the appearance, suggestion, or claim of a universal belief in a selfhood apart from God, of a universe apart from God, and of a selfhood and universe subject to material and mental laws.

This Universe Is Governed by Principle

Can you believe that there is God *and* sickness, too? Where would God be while someone is suffering? Human parents would never permit a child to suffer from a disease if they could prevent it. Would you let your child suffer? Then why do you think God would? It cannot be. In reality, there never has been a sick person or a dead one. Everybody who has ever lived from the beginning of all time is still alive—it could not be otherwise. Unless you accept this truth, you are really an atheist and believe that the world sprang up out of dust, that it is going to return to dust, and that there is no God.

But how can you believe that when you observe the law of like begetting like in operation: apples always coming from apple trees, cabbages coming from cabbage plants? That cannot be accidental; there must be a law. This is not an accidental world. There must be a principle behind it, and that principle is God. If there is a principle, is there ever an exception to the principle? In our system of mathematics two times two is four always, and there is never any exception to that. Does anything grow on apple trees but apples, or on orange trees but oranges?

There is a Principle governing the universe, and because there is a Principle, a divine Law, nothing is ever outside Its government or control, not any more than do the notes of the scale—do, re, mi, fa, sol, la, ti—change in their relationship to one another. No one note has ever crowded another off the scale. No one note has ever infringed upon another. No one note has ever taken anything away from another note.

It is exactly the same with the digits nought, one, two, three, four, five, six, seven, eight, and nine. They never get out of their rightful places; not one of them has ever taken anything from one of the others; not one has ever crowded the other out or drawn from another. Cooperation? Yes, they have cooperated for the common good.

If that is true of mathematics and true of music, how can it be other than true of man who was given dominion over mathematics and music? So, there never has been a man who crowded another man off the earth; there never has been a man who crowded another man out of his business. Never! Those pictures are a part of universal hypnotism, and if we can be made to believe that there is a mortal, material universe, we, too, are a part of this hypnotism. Hypnotism is the error, and we are the ones who have to correct it through the understanding that one with God is a majority. The moment a person knows the truth, or can turn to someone higher in consciousness who can know the truth for him, that "one on God's side is a majority," and that breaks the spell.

"Go, and Sin No More"

The mesmerism may be broken, but that does not mean that the dehypnotized person cannot soon get himself back into it again. If he does not conform to the higher vision, nothing is going to stop him from slipping right back into the same sin, the same disease, or a different one. Jesus said, "Neither do I condemn thee: go, and sin no more." In other words: "I release you and give you your freedom through my understanding of your spiritual nature, but do not go back and indulge in mortality again." If a person who is healed does not change his mode of life, that is, if he goes back and "sins" again, he may find that a worse thing will come upon him.

The world misunderstands the meaning of the word "sin." It means not only getting drunk, committing adultery, or stealing: there is much more to sin than that. Sin is really the acceptance of a material universe. Just going back to the belief that there are human beings is the sin that throws a person back into disease and sin again. What the world might call sin—stealing, lying, cheating, and adultery—is of the same nature as disease: it is just another form of hypnotism.

Hypnotism Is the
Substance of All Discord

There is no difference between the hell called poverty and that called war, disease, or sin. One of them is no worse than another. They are all forms of one thing, and that one thing is hypnotism. In one man, hypnotism appears as some sinful thing or thought; in another, it appears as a diseased condition or thought; and in still another, it appears as poverty. The particular form makes no difference; it is all hypnotism. Take away the hypnotism, and none of these things would be there. There is only one error, and that is hypnotism.

If we can be induced to give treatments to persons—to treat them for nerves or for a mental cause for a physical disease, to treat them for resentment, hatred, jealousy, or anger, or if we can be made to treat them for cancer or consumption—we are not in the practice of spiritual healing: we are in *materia medica* because we are treating effects, whether the effect is a sin, a disease, or poverty, and if we do get rid of it, two more effects lift their heads.

Until we lay the ax at the root of the tree, which is hypnotism, we do not come out of the mortal or material state of consciousness. When we are able to see through the hypnotism, regardless of the name or nature of the sin, disease, or lack, our patient or student will experience harmony, health, wholeness, and completeness. If his trouble is nerves, he finds himself rid of nerves; if his belief is unemployment, he finds himself employed; if his claim is disease, he finds himself well. Why? Because of the practitioner's ability to see through the claim of hypnotism and realize God as the principle of all that is.

Many times, however, even after a student understands hypnotism to be operating as the suggestion or appearance, he still believes there is a real condition to be destroyed. That is when we hear such expressions as, "Look what hypnotism is doing to me." But hypnotism is not an actual thing or condition. Hypnotism cannot produce water on the desert or snakes in the flowerpot. Hypnotism is itself no thing, no form, no cause, and no effect. Recognizing any form or appearance of error as hypnotism and then dismissing it without any further concern is the correct way to handle all error.

Meditate on this idea of hypnotism as the substance of every form of the mortal or material universe that is appearing to you. When you see sin, disease, lack, and limitation, remember it is hypnotism presenting itself to you as what is called evil form. But then when you see beauty all around, the mountains, ocean, and sunshine, remember that these, too, are forms of hypnotism, only this time appearing to you as good forms.

This does not mean that we are not to enjoy the good of human existence, but rather that we are to enjoy it for what it is—not as something real, in and of itself, but because the reality, that which underlies all good, is spiritual and must therefore be spiritually discerned. We enjoy the forms of good, knowing them to be temporary forms, not something to be stored up, not something to be put in bank vaults, but something to be enjoyed, and then we go on each day letting the manna fall afresh.

When confronted with the negative aspects of hypnotism, that is, the forms of sin, disease, lack, and limitation, the most important point to remember is that we are not to be fooled by them, not to be fooled into trying to reform evil or sinful persons, but always quickly to remember: "Oh, no! This is hypnotism appearing in still another form, hypnotism which, in and of itself, cannot be the substance, law, cause, or effect of any form of reality." Such a practice enables you to become a spiritual healer.

Never Try to Change
a Person or a Condition

As you go further in the work and, through meditation, are able to rise to a point where you are above this world, then you will know me as I am, and I will know you as you are. That is how healings take place, and that is why I caution our students not to tell people that they must correct themselves, not to refuse patients because they do not seem to be doing what they think is right. That has nothing to do with the student. He must go within and see the person he is trying to help as God made him, and then the patient will soon conform "to the pattern shewed to thee in the mount."

The world is hypnotized by person, place, and thing to such a degree that a good person, a good place, and a good thing become so pleasant and comfortable that everybody wants to enjoy these effects, and they do not want to go any higher than that. Such material pleasures and enjoyments cannot be a permanent dispensation, however, because no matter how much good a person may have, he still fluctuates between the pairs of opposites.

So again, I say this to you: If you can be made to treat a person in an attempt to change him or give him more of this world's good, or if you can be made to fear war, a depression, or an atomic bomb, you are hypnotized. It is only a question, then, of what date will be placed on your tombstone. If, however, you can catch this vision, when the time comes for you to leave this world, you will step out into a transitional experience which will be higher and better than this one.

You cannot treat a person; you cannot treat a condition. To do that would be like trying to treat the snakes appearing in the flowerpot and saying, "I've got to get rid of my three snakes. As soon as I get rid of them, I'll be able to study better." Do you see how foolish that is? There are not any snakes, so you are never going to get rid of them. All you have to do is to get rid of the hypnotism!

When you really know and believe that—not just believe words—you will no longer have to study truth because the only purpose in studying truth is to learn that hypnotism is the only error, and when you have learned that, there is nothing more to study. All the rest is to be lived within your own being.

The minute you try to change or improve a disease or condition, you yourself are in the hypnotism because there is no disease or condition apart from the mesmerism or the hypnotism. To be ensnared, then, into trying to handle the condition would be but to make the whole situation worse.

Those who are reading or studying truth or who are using truth for healing, for supply, or for some other purpose will find that the more their minds are fixed on getting rid of the condition or on getting the healing, the more are their minds in the mirage of error. You must see that there is no human demonstration to make. There is only one demonstration, and that is gaining the realization of God.

When you have the realization of God, you have all: you have supply; you have immortal life, eternality, and infinity. You cannot demonstrate a home, a companion, a divorce, or a job; you can only demonstrate the presence of God and that includes whatever the nature of the outward demonstration is to be.

There Is No God "And"

Recognizing the hypnotism includes the demonstration of getting rid of whatever form it might take: the water on the road, the snakes in the flowerpot, or the cancer. But you cannot get rid of these separate and apart from getting rid of the hypnotism. Neither can you make a demonstration of home, employment, or health separate and apart from achieving the conscious realization of God, because there is no demonstration of good separate and apart from God.

There is no use treating person, place, or thing because all there is to error is hypnotism. There is no use seeking a demonstration of person, thing, or condition because there is no demonstration separate and apart from the realization of God. The realization of God includes all demonstrations. "Seek ye first the kingdom of God, and his righteousness; and all these things shall be added unto you."

The important point to understand is that it is the same on the positive side as on the negative. On the positive side, it is demonstrating the consciousness of the presence of God; on the negative side, it is realizing that no matter what the form of error is, it is hypnotism, and hypnotism alone, which has no substance, law, cause, reality, or effect. These are the two sides of the picture.

The entire basis of The Infinite Way teaching is that there is not God *and*. There is not God *and* health, or God *and* strength, or God *and* immortality, or God *and* activity, or God *and* supply. There is only God manifesting *as*. You can take a block of mahogany, and out of it make a chair, a table, and a bench. But you do not have mahogany *and* a table *and* a chair *and* a bench: you have mahogany manifested or expressed *as* those pieces of furniture.

Therefore, when you think of God as the substance of the universe, you do not have God, the Substance, *and* a variety of forms: you have God appearing or formed as these forms, manifested and expressed as form. That is why, if you demonstrate God, you demonstrate every form as which God appears. You demonstrate God as health, as harmony, as immortality, and as supply. You cannot demonstrate God *and* these things, and you cannot demonstrate these things separate and apart from God because they are all God Itself formed.

There Is No Hypnotism "And"

This idea of no separation between the substance of a thing and the thing itself can also be applied to an understanding of all error as hypnotism. There is not hypnotism *and* a disease. There is not hypnotism *and* lack and limitation; there is not hypnotism *and* sin and death. There is only hypnotism appearing as these pictures. You cannot get rid of the sin, disease, or death separate and apart from the hypnotism, but when you have rid yourself of hypnotism, you are rid of all its various forms. The way to remove the effects of hypnotism is to understand hypnotism, not as a thing, but as no thing, no power, no presence.

Here you have the secret of living. When, through the senses, you observe life as it seems to be—as you see, hear, taste, touch, or smell it—you understand immediately that this is the product of hypnotism. Through your spiritual sense, however, you discern that right where this human, material, or physical sense seems to be is the spiritual, eternal, and immortal creation.

If you were to see a so-called evil appearance, a sinful, sick, dying, or dead appearance, you would probably be tempted immediately to know some truth that you hope would change the picture, or to think some thought that would heal, correct, improve, or reform it; whereas, if you saw normal human good, normal human wealth, harmony, wholeness, or prosperity, you would most likely accept that picture at its face value.

Hypnotism is just as much hypnotism when it appears as good as when it appears as evil. When you come into a state of life, however, where you can look at the harmonious human appearance and recognize it as hypnotism or appearance or suggestion, and when you can look at the inharmonious or discordant human picture and recognize it as the product of the same hypnotism, as appearance or suggestion, then you have arrived at a point in consciousness in which you will not try to improve, heal, or correct the erroneous picture, nor experience undue satisfaction over the harmonious picture. That is because you will know through your spiritual sense that, regardless of the picture or the nature of its appearance, right there is spiritual reality and harmony, right there eternal and immortal being is. So you will make no mental effort to correct, heal, or improve it. And with that ability to refrain from all attempts to heal, correct, or improve, you will have demonstrated the consciousness of God's allness.

If you can know that the harmonious human appearances are no more real than the inharmonious or discordant ones and if you can know that inharmonious, discordant, sick, sinful, dying human appearances are no more real than harmonious or healthful appearances, then you have arrived at a state of consciousness that spiritually discerns harmony right where any form or human appearance may be.

When you have become accustomed to the idea of observing the harmonious human appearances and the inharmonious human appearances with the same degree of unconcern, you will know that you have arrived at a state of spiritual consciousness in which you see that which is invisible, hear that which is inaudible, and know that which is unknowable. This is Christ-consciousness.

Across the Desk

In March, we traveled to California, and in May, we start on another trip through the United States and Europe. Again, we will experience the joy of meeting with those who have dedicated themselves to God.

We are ever-mindful of the many revelators of spiritual wisdom whose lives have been consecrated to God's purpose, and of those who have devoted themselves to carrying on their work. Even to think of Zarathustra, Lao-Tzu, Buddha, Jesus the Christ, and Shankara is to find oneself on holy ground. There are many others, too, who inspire us because we witness the nature of their consecration.

There is another form of dedication which we meet in the lives of those who have surrendered their personal sense of life to give themselves, yes, dedicate themselves to the cause of freedom, and this is a consecration to loving one's neighbor as himself. These unselfed souls brought forth the freedom of England, France, Holland, Switzerland, countries in North and South America, as well as others throughout the world.

Many now are devoting themselves to worthy causes in different parts of the world. Some have given themselves to youth in the work of the YMCA and the YWCA, the Boy

Scouts and Girl Scouts, to the poor through their work in the Salvation Army, and to the suffering by carrying food and clothing to friendly and enemy countries. Such movements as Care and the Peace Corps demonstrate love in concrete form.

This dedication to God, expressed as consecration to our neighbors' needs, ennobles the lives of those who are called and furnishes inspiration to the rest of us so that we, too, may rise above the deadness and dullness of human living. Real living begins only when inspiration enters. Self-completeness is attained only in giving and serving. Freedom is attained in consecration, and peace is found in dedication.

When the Spirit of God touches us, there follows an unrest, a disquiet, a lack of satisfaction with ordinary human experience, and this persists until we find ourselves serving God in our neighbor and resting in Him.

JOEL GOLDSMITH RECORDED CLASSES CORRESPONDING TO THE CHAPTERS OF THIS BOOK

Many of Joel Goldsmith's books, including this one, are based on his recorded classwork, which has been preserved in tape, CD, and MP3 formats by the Infinite Way Office in Moreno Valley, CA.

The listing below shows the classes related to each chapter of this book. For example, "#159-1 1956 Chicago Closed Class 2:1" means:

The recording number is 159, Side 1 (**#159-1**).

The recording is from the **1956 Chicago Closed Class**.

The recording is Tape 2, Side 1 for the 1956 Chicago Closed Class **(2:1)**.

1. THE NEW HORIZON

In the 1956 May *Infinite Way Letter*, Joel calls this chapter "the practitioner's chapter."

2. BREAK THE FETTERS THAT BIND YOU

#241-1: 1958 Maui Open Class 1:1

3. MARCH: PROTECTION

No tape source known

4. CONTEMPLATION DEVELOPS THE BEHOLDER

#369-2: 1960 Maui Work 4:2

5. The Relationship of Oneness

#612-2: 1951 Second Portland Series 12:2
#608-2: 1951 Second Portland Series 8:2 (or try 9:1 or 9:2)
#1004-1: 1952 First Class of 1952 3:1
#1004-2: 1952 First Class of 1952 3:2
#68-1: 1954 Honolulu Lecture Series 4:1
#68-2: 1954 Honolulu Lecture Series 4:2
#69-1: 1954 Honolulu Lecture Series 5:1
#69-2: 1954 Honolulu Lecture Series 5:2
#70-1: 1954 Honolulu Lecture Series 6:1
#49-2: 1953 First New York Closed Class 2:2
#48-1: 1953 First New York Closed Class 1:1
#51-1: 1953 First New York Closed Class 4:1
#240-2: 1958 First Maui Lectures 2:2

6. Introduction

7. Love Thy Neighbor

#620-1: 1953 Second New York Closed Class 1:1
#620-2: 1953 Second New York Closed Class 1:2
#108: 1955 Chicago Private Class 2 (*no specific side cited*)
#125: 1955 Kailua Study Group 16 (*no specific side cited*)
#17: 1952 Honolulu Closed Class 4 (*no specific side cited*)
#15-1: 1952 Honolulu Closed Class 2:1
#617-2: 1952 Second Seattle Closed Class 1:2
#618-2: 1952 Second Seattle Closed Class 2:2

8. God Is One

#23-2: 1953 New Hawaiian Series 4:2

9. No *And!*

#12-1: 1952 Honolulu Class, Series One 2:1

BIBLE REFERENCES
(BY FIRST LINE)

A

B – C – D

E – F

J – K – L

Joint heir to all the heavenly riches ....Romans 8:17

Judge not after appearances;
judge righteous judgement ....John 7:24

Lean not unto thine own understanding ....Proverbs 3:5

Let the dead bury their dead ....Luke 9:60

Live and move and have our being ....Acts 17:28

Lo, I am with you always ....Matthew 28:20

Loose him and let him go ....John 11:44

Lord, even the devils ....Luke 10:17

M

Man shall not live by bread alone ....Matthew 4:4

Man whose breath is in his nostrils ....Isaiah 2:22

Many mansions ....John 14:2

My grace is sufficient ....2 Corinthians 12:9

My kingdom is not of this world ....John 18:36

My peace give I unto you ....John 14:27

N – O – P

Neither do I condemn thee, go and sin no more ....John 8:11

Neither lo here nor lo there ....Luke 17:21

None of these things move me ....Acts 20:24

Nothing can enter that defileth or maketh a lie .....Revelation 21:27

Peace I leave with you ....John 14:27

R – S

T

U – W – Y

Made in the USA
Monee, IL
17 April 2024

57069166R00085